BUKOWSKI IN PICTURES

By the same author

Fred & Rose
Charles Bukowski: Locked in the Arms of a Crazy Life

HOWARD SOUNES

BUKOWSKI
IN PICTURES

REBEL
inc.

First published in Great Britain in 2000 by
Rebel Inc, an imprint of
Canongate Books Ltd, 14 High Street,
Edinburgh EH1 1TE

10 9 8 7 6 5 4 3 2 1

Rebel Inc series editor: Kevin Williamson
www.rebelinc.net

British Library Cataloguing-in-Publication Data
A catalogue record for this book is available on
request from the British Library

ISBN 1 84195 008 4

Set in Adobe Jenson and Bell Gothic

Printed and bound by LEGO, Italy

Acknowledgements   ix

Author's Note   xi

Introduction   1

THIS GRAVEYARD ABOVE THE GROUND   21

WHAT A LIFE   29

LOST YEARS   37

JANE, WITH ALL THE LOVE I HAD WHICH   45
WAS NOT ENOUGH

EAST HOLLYWOOD   57

SHIT JOBS   71

LOVE IS A DOG FROM HELL   91

HUMANITY, YOU NEVER HAD IT FROM   111
THE BEGINNING

LIVING ON LUCK   125

HORSELESS DAYS AND GOODBYE SMILES   143

SOURCE NOTES ON THE TEXT   154

Later famous for gambling on horse flesh, here is a unique photograph of Charles Bukowski in the saddle. The picture was taken in California in 1926, probably on his sixth birthday, and sent by Bukowski's mother Kate to her parents in Germany. She informed them in an accompanying letter that the pony was called Tommy, adding: 'Time goes by so quickly … I can scarcely believe I have such a big boy.'
(PHOTOGRAPH COURTESY OF KARL FETT)

the bluebird

there's a bluebird in my heart that
wants to get out
but I'm too tough for him,
I say, stay in there, I'm not going
to let anybody see
you.

there's a bluebird in my heart that
wants to get out
but I pour whiskey on him and inhale
cigarette smoke
and the whores and the bartenders
and the grocery clerks
never know that
he's
in there.

there's a bluebird in my heart that
wants to get out
but I'm too tough for him,
I say,
stay down, do you want to mess
me up?
you want to screw up the
works?
you want to blow my book sales in
Europe?

there's a bluebird in my heart that
wants to get out
but I'm too clever, I only let him out
at night sometimes
when everybody's asleep.
I say, I know that you're there,
so don't be
sad.

then I put him back,
but he's singing a little
in there, I haven't quite let him
die
and we sleep together like
that
with our
secret pact
and it's nice enough to
make a man
weep, but I don't
weep, do
you?

Charles Bukowski

Black Sparrow Press on the occasion of
Copyright © 1991 by Charles Bukowski.

Published November 1991 for the friends of the
the San Francisco Bay Area Book Festival.

Thank you to these relatives of Charles Bukowski: FrancEyE, the mother of his daughter; cousin Karl Heinrich Fett, of Andernach, Germany (and to Matthew Davis for translating); Leah Belle Wilson, whose cousin Barbara Frye was Bukowski's first wife; and cousin Katherine Wood of California.

The following friends, acquaintances and correspondents of Bukowski allowed their personal photographs and memorabilia to appear in this book: John Bennett; John William Corrington's widow, Joyce; Brad Darby and his ex-wife Tina Ewing; Al Purdy; Steve Richmond; Jory Sherman; Joan Jobe Smith; Concepcion Tadeo; John Thomas; Louise 'Gypsy Lou' Webb and Joe Wolberg.

Bukowski's former girlfriends shared their pictures, love letters and memories. Thank you to: Joanna Bull, Linda King, Ann Menebroker, Amber O'Neil, Jo Jo Planteen and Liza Williams.

Thank you to the professional photographers who contributed their work: Robert Gumpert; Gottfried Helnwein, and his agent Katya Kashkooli

at Modernism; Don Klein; Tony Lane; and Gerard Malanga. Thank you to: Al Berlinski of Sun Dog Press, Northville, Michigan; Roger Myers at The University of Arizona Library, Tucson, Arizona; David Tambo, Head of Special Collections at the University of California at Santa Barbara; Greg Spradling at Roswell High School, Roswell, New Mexico; and Brenda I. Galloway-Wright at Temple University, Philadelphia, Pennsylvania.

Permission to reproduce 'Aftermath of a Lengthy Rejection Slip', the cover of *Harlequin* and the covers of Bukowski's early chapbooks has been sought.

Finally, thank you to the illustrators Dave Geiser and R. Crumb.

The book was art directed by James Hutcheson and designed by Barrie Tullett. The photographs, artwork and other images were collected from a wide variety of sources including Charles Bukowski's relatives, his former girlfriends, fellow poets, university libraries and professional photographers.

ACKNOWLEDGEMENTS

LEFT
Afternoon sunlight streams through the door of Charles Bukowski's rented bungalow in Hollywood, California. The year is 1976 and he has recently published his second novel, Factotum.
(PHOTOGRAPH BY TONY LANE)

FACING PAGE
Printed in 1991, 'the bluebird' was published as part of the San Francisco Bay Area Book Festival.
(PHOTOGRAPH BY DON KLEIN)

During the researching and writing of my biography of Charles Bukowski – *Charles Bukowski: Locked in the Arms of a Crazy Life* – I interviewed the surviving members of his family, most of his former friends and lovers, his publishers and fellow writers. As I travelled through Germany, where Bukowski was born, and the United States of America, where he lived all his adult life, I gathered personal documents, unpublished letters, and what became a large collection of previously unpublished photographs. Photographs would be an important part of the biography, partly because Bukowski is almost as famous as a personality as he is a writer, and his singular looks were an integral part of his persona. The extreme case of acne he suffered as a youth, followed by years of alcoholism, left him with an alarming face of scarred and swollen flesh. He *looked* like a man who been through brutal and dangerous experiences. A not uncommon reaction upon first seeing a picture of Bukowski is to recoil – people think that he looks weird, even grotesque. Indeed, Bukowski himself was convinced of his ugliness. Yet as he matured, it seems to me, his face came to have the grandeur of a monumental carving. With his bushy eyebrows raised and his thin lips slightly upturned, his forbidding appearance could soften to radiate wisdom, honesty and a mischievous good humour. He became a wonderful-looking old man.

Photographs also added information to the story of Bukowski's life. The pictures of his reviled father show a sour-faced man, apparently as unpleasant as the character described in Bukowski's poems and stories. The pictures of Bukowski as a boy, looking sad and frightened, add credence to his accounts of a miserable childhood. Photographs of Bukowski's first wife, Barbara Frye – the first pictures of her to be published – clearly show the physical deformity Bukowski wrote about in *Notes of a Dirty Old Man*. The face of Jane Cooney Baker, the lover against whom Bukowski judged all women, appears like a ghost. We can see the melancholy face of the woman who inspired his great poetry anthology, *The Days Run Away Like Wild Horses Over the Hills*. Conversely, photographs contradict the mythology Bukowski created for himself. A series of photographs of a smartly dressed Bukowski, taken in 1947, posing with his parents at home in Los Angeles, puts a question mark against his assertion that he was a skid row bum throughout the 1940s.

I made a particular point of collecting photographs of Bukowski's family and his friends, because he based so many characters in his writing on people he knew. Henry, or 'Hank' Chinaski was, of course, only a slight variation on Charles 'Hank' Bukowski himself, and Chinaski's parents were close to his actual parents. Several relatives were used for material, including Bukowski's Uncle John about whom he wrote memorably in the poem 'the bones of my uncle'. School friends James Haddox and William Mulllinax inspired the characters of Jimmy and 'Baldy', Chinaski's two friends in the novel *Ham on Rye*. Friends from adult life were also used. Actor Mickey Rourke inspired the Jack Bledsoe character in *Hollywood*. Bukowski's publisher, John Martin, became John Barton in *Pulp*.

Bukowski seemed to derive glee from creating shrewish female characters based on the women in his life; some former girlfriends say he made caricatures of them. When he was dating the sculptress Linda King in the mid-1970s, he wrote to John Martin that he was, 'making a study on [Linda]. If I ever get it down right some day you'll see the female exposed as she has never been exposed.' Sure enough, Linda became Lydia in the novel *Women*. As you look through this book, you will meet the real people who inspired all the familiar Bukowski characters.

He wrote vividly about where he lived and where

Bukowski with his mother Kate in California, 1926. She dressed her son in a style fashionable in her native country of Germany.
(PHOTOGRAPH COURTESY OF JOE WOLBERG)

could form the core of a second, complementary book. The core collection has been enlarged since the publication of the biography, as former friends of Bukowski gave me further access to their archives. Artists R. Crumb and Dave Geiser supplied illustrations. I approached professional photographers who worked with Bukowski – including San Francisco-based Robert Gumpert, the distinguished German photographer Gottfried Helnwein, former *Rolling Stone* art director Tony Lane and Andy Warhol's former assistant Gerard Malanga – and they added to the project. The result is *Bukowski in Pictures*.

he worked, work being very important in his writing. So as well as collecting photographs of people, I collected pictures of places, taking simple pocket-camera photographs of my own when I found a building still standing that had some significance in Bukowski's life. There were many places in Los Angeles to visit. Naturally I wanted to know what the post office of Bukowski's eponymous novel was like. When I visited the Terminal Annex, next to Union Station in downtown LA, I saw that it was a huge, forbidding factory. Seeing this enormous building helped me appreciate one of Bukowski's great achievements – after years of mindless manual labour he left the post office at the age of forty-nine to become a successful writer. Bukowski was a man who made his dreams real.

When research on the biography was complete, I had a large collection of photographs from which seventy-two were selected to illustrate *Charles Bukowski: Locked in the Arms of a Crazy Life*. There was no space for more. It became clear that the remaining pictures, combined with artwork, extracts from manuscripts and rare personal documents,

The text is primarily intended to aid appreciation of the photographs. The introduction sets out the essential facts of Bukowski's biography in chronological order, from his birth in 1920 to his death in 1994. There is, however, new material here because new sources of information have emerged since the biography was completed. Most notably, the Federal Bureau of Investigations in Washington DC has released a copy of Bukowski's FBI file, a surprising document revealing that FBI Director J. Edgar Hoover and his agents made extensive investigations into Bukowski's life in the 1960s. Information from this file is published here for the first time.

Howard Sounes
London, 2000

Andernach is a small, picturesque town in Germany, north of Frankfurt on the left bank of the River Rhine, a place of cobbled streets, ancient stone buildings and fragments of fortifications dating back to the middle ages. Charles Bukowski was born here as Heinrich Karl Bukowski on 16 August, 1920. His father, Henry, was an American soldier serving as a sergeant in the United States army of occupation following the end of World War I. Bukowski's mother was a seamstress by the name of Katharina Fett, daughter of a local musician. She married Henry one month before giving birth to their only child. Around this time, Henry was demobilised from the army and went to work for the Rents, Requisitions and Claims Service in Germany and then as a self-employed building contractor. He probably would have settled if not for the collapse of the German economy in 1923, bringing out-of-control inflation and unemployment. When Little Heinrich was two years and eight months old – on 18 April, 1923 – Henry took his family to the United States of America.

The Bukowski family entered the United States at the port city of Baltimore, where they stayed for several months, before travelling to California, where Henry Bukowski had been born and raised. After a short stay in Pasadena with his parents, Leonard and Emilie Bukowski, themselves German-speaking émigrés from Eastern Europe, Henry and his family settled in the rapidly expanding city of Los Angeles. To make themselves appear less foreign in their new home, they softened the harsh European pronunciation of their surname and anglicised their first names. Katharina became Kate and Little Heinrich became Henry Jnr.

The family lived in a series of suburban houses before settling in a large, recently built detached bungalow at 2122 Longwood Avenue. Henry Bukowski got a job as a milkman, delivering milk by horse and cart. It was a job he felt was beneath him.

He was a surly, unhappy man who considered himself superior to the people he delivered to, and better than the neighbourhood he lived in. But he did not have the qualifications to gain skilled work. Indeed, in the 1930s, when America was reeling from the aftermath of the Great Depression, Henry was unemployed for months. The family was so impoverished they almost lost their home.

By Bukowski's own account in his poetry and prose, in letters to friends and in interviews, his father was a brutal and sadistic man who would beat him for the smallest misdemeanour. Henry made the boy cut the lawns, front and back, every Saturday. If one solitary blade of grass was sticking up above the lawn by the end of the day, his father would take him into the bathroom and thrash him with a razor strop. Bukowski's mother watched impassively. When the little boy wailed for mercy, she said his father knew best. Bukowski hated his father, and lost all respect for his mother.

When Bukowski was thirteen, his skin erupted in a mass of boils, a case of acne so severe that his parents, who were ashamed of the way he looked, took him to the Los Angeles County Hospital. Bukowski claimed the doctors treated him as a freak, testing out painful new procedures without consideration for his feelings. The pain of having the boils on his face, chest and back drilled with an electric needle was, in fact, excruciating, but Bukowski refused to cry.

He learned the value of self-control by enduring the beatings from his father. After the first few years, he suffered his beatings in silence. This apparently unnerved Henry Bukowski who stopped the punishments. By enduring pain the boy achieved a sort of victory, and stoicism in the face of adversity became an integral part of his character. In later life Bukowski would rarely lose his temper, except when very drunk. He took the view that he was going to be disappointed and hurt by most people – as he said,

When he lived at Carlton Way in Hollywood in the mid-1970s Bukowski wrote a column for the Los Angeles Free Press *entitled 'Notes of a Dirty Old Man'. One night when he was drinking with neighbours Brad and Tina Darby he told them that any writer worth his words should be prepared to eat his own words. 'So he ate the whole* Free Press *and then threw it up over my carpeting,' says Tina Darby.*
(PHOTOGRAPH BY TINA EWING, FORMERLY DARBY)

'Most human beings just aren't worth a shit' – so there was no point losing his dignity.

The acne was so bad, and treatment so intensive, that Bukowski was excused the first semester of high school. He received regular treatments at LA County and travelled by street-car between the hospital and his home, his face sometimes wrapped in bandages like Boris Karloff in the film, *The Mummy*, which had recently been released. Little wonder children stared at him. When he did not have an appointment at the hospital, there was little to do at home. Bukowski visited the local public library where he started to read novels. He devoured the works of D. H. Lawrence, Ernest Hemingway, Sinclair Lewis and John Dos Passos before moving onto the great nineteenth-century Russian writers. Literature was comfort and joy to a lonely boy, as he wrote in, *Ham on Rye*:

> Words weren't dull, words were things that could make your mind hum. If you read them and let yourself feel the magic, you could live without pain, with hope, no matter what happened to you.

Bukowski enrolled at Susan Miller Dorsey High School in the September of 1936, around the time he started to take a precocious interest in alcohol. The teenaged Bukowski was so disfigured by acne that he looked much older than his years and was readily served in bars. He started sneaking out at night, climbing back in through his bedroom window only when his money was gone. One night Bukowski came home drunk and vomited over the living room rug.

INSET

A young Charles Bukowski on a day out with his parents at Santa Monica Beach, California.
(COURTESY OF KARL FETT)

RIGHT

This is a rare photograph of Bukowski during the early 1950s, when he was living with girlfriend Jane Cooney Baker. The picture, probably taken by Jane, shows Bukowski relaxing on a beach with a dog they owned. On the back of the photograph Bukowski wrote these words: '…long ago on a deserted beach with a fine and beautiful dog'. Bukowski was later cruel to the dog, something he regretted for the rest of his life.
(COURTESY OF THE UNIVERSITY OF ARIZONA LIBRARY)

His father tried to push Bukowski's face into the vomit, like a dog. Bukowski retaliated by punching his father. His outraged mother slapped, scratched and clawed her son's face until he was bloody.

These wretched experiences hardened Bukowski, at least on the outside, and he bullied the few friends he had, boys including William 'Baldy' Mullinax and Jimmy Haddox. However, most of Bukowski's fellow students saw through his surly, aggressive demeanour. Hank, as he was known from childhood, was pitied because of his skin problem and the few fellow students who remember him say their abiding impression is of a painfully shy youth. He could barely manage to say hello to students outside his immediate circle; he hardly ever joined in conversations, and he never had girlfriends, although he craved the attention of girls.

In September 1937, he transferred schools, moving from Susan Miller Dorsey High to Los Angeles High School in the affluent Hancock Park neighbourhood. LA High was one of the elite public schools in the city. The journey to school was longer and less convenient and Bukowski was probably transferred because of the snobbish aspirations of his father. If he felt awkward at his old school, Bukowski felt like a positive freak at LA High, where the students appeared to lead golden lives. Not only were most of the students good-looking, in Bukowski's estimation, most were from affluent families. Boys and girls seemed at ease with each other, going on dates, to dances downtown, to movie theatres and to the beach. Bukowski, who considered himself physically repulsive, was not included in these activities. Most of the time he was ignored by fellow students. When they did notice him, they mocked his strange looks and lack of confidence. There seemed to be nothing attractive or special about Hank Bukowski. He did not even show an emerging talent for writing. The school had a poetry club, but Bukowski was not a member. Academically, he was a 'C' average student who did just enough to graduate. After leaving school, in 1939, he was quickly forgotten by most of the pupils and teachers.

After working briefly in a department store, Bukowski attempted to further his education by enrolling at Los Angeles City College (LACC). He was as much of an outsider here as he had been at high school, but rather than trying to ingratiate himself to make friends, Bukowski seems to have decided to revel in his unpopularity, creating a negative persona for himself. It was not that people did not want to be friends with him; he began to give the impression that *he* did not want their friendship, that he was a loner who did not need anybody. Part of this act was to flirt with deeply unpopular far right politics. Bukowski caused outrage among his teachers and fellow pupils by speaking up for Adolf Hitler. He later excused his behaviour saying he had never been interested in politics of any sort, but enjoyed being provocative. Aside from this, Bukowski's brief time at LACC was unremarkable. His grades were average to poor, and the college was threatening to withdraw his state scholarship when he dropped out in 1941.

He was downtown looking for a job when he went into the Los Angeles Public Library on West 5th Street. It was here that Bukowski discovered a novel that changed his life. The book was *Ask the Dust* by Italian-American writer John Fante. It concerns a young, aspiring writer, Arturo Bandini, who goes to live in the Bunker Hill district of downtown LA in order to find love, and other experiences, which he might write about. Bukowski identified strongly with the character of Bandini and was excited that Bunker Hill was a real place, just across the road from the library. He rented a room in one of the decrepit apartment houses on Bunker

Hill, beginning to think he might become a writer. He worked at a series of manual jobs in factories and the railroad yards next to Union Station. He drank in the local bars and began to compose short stories on the typewriter his parents bought for him when he was at college. After a few months on Bunker Hill, Bukowski packed a bag and set out across the USA by bus to collect further experiences so that, like Arturo Bandini, he too would have something to write about

The following years became a central part of the self-created mythology of Bukowski's life. He called this period his 'lost years' or his 'ten-year-drunk', a decade when he trudged back and forth across the country, drinking heavily, working manual jobs and living in rented rooms. The people he kept company with were bums, bar keeps and prostitutes, although

Bukowski and his 'Volks'.
(PHOTOGRAPH BY JOE WOLBERG)

he was solitary by nature, and spent as much time as possible alone. These were the raw experiences he used for many of his most famous short stories, for his second novel, *Factotum*, and for the screenplay of the 1987 movie, *Barfly*. In reality, Bukowski's life on the road was brief. He left Los Angeles for relatively short periods of time – two years at most – and between trips he lived with his parents. A series of photographs taken at Longwood Avenue in July 1947, the middle of his supposed barfly years, show Bukowski posing in the back garden of the house with his parents. He is wearing a suit and tie and gives every appearance of being a model son. This does not detract from the essential truth and power of Bukowski's writing, but it is clear he embellished his life to provide material for his work, taking episodes of hardship and stretching these out as if they were the whole story. The real events of his early life and the literature he wrote became tightly entangled, creating the mythology of Bukowski as a kind of hobo poet. This was never the whole truth. Bukowski was careful with money, keeping savings in the bank for most of his life. He was not a great traveller and there is no evidence he was ever homeless. Indeed, apart his wanderings in the 1940s, Bukowski rarely strayed beyond the few square miles of central Los Angeles he had known since childhood.

Bukowski began writing in earnest when he was travelling in the early 1940s. At first he wrote short stories which he mailed to the New York magazines. After many rejections, he was first published in the spring of 1944 in *Story*. Bukowski decided his pen name should be Charles Bukowski. He did not want to use his first name, Henry, because it reminded him of his father, and Charles sounded more sophisticated than Hank. It was a tremendously exciting moment in his life, and he travelled to New York to see the magazine on the news stands. But Bukowski was disappointed. His humorous short story about trying to get published, 'Aftermath of a Lengthy Rejection Slip', had been published as part of the end pages of as a novelty item, and his name was not on the contents page. Bukowski believed he had been made a fool of, and was so discouraged he almost gave up writing.

World War II was raging and Bukowski had to register for military service. His problems with the draft board became a story he told many times in his poetry and prose. New light has been shed on these events by documents that form part of a file the FBI compiled in 1968 when Bukowski was investigated, as a government employee (a humble postal worker), for writing 'obscene' articles in the underground press. By Bukowski's own account, he had been willing to serve his country during World War II. But the FBI file reveals that Bukowski wrote to the draft board prior to induction stating he, 'did not have any intentions of reporting for induction due to his personal philosophy, and [that he] wanted to know just what action [the draft board] would take in view of that information.' There are no details of what this 'personal philosophy' was, but throughout his life Bukowski was a nonconformist without religious or political beliefs, except when he wanted to say something for shock value, like admiring Hitler, and he did not share the jingoistic patriotism of many Americans. He was informed that unless he reported to the draft board, he might go to jail. Bukowski dutifully reported for induction. According to the file, Bukowski was then disqualified for military service as 4-F ('Rejected for military service; physical, mental or moral reasons.') He wrote about this many times, always stating that the reason he was rejected was that the army psychiatrist decided he was 'psycho', due to 'extreme sensitivity'. The FBI file indicates Bukowski was, in fact, rejected on physical grounds, although the specific problem is not recorded.

Bukowski still had to report to the draft board because there was a possibility he might, in the future, be considered fit to serve. He was also obliged to notify the board whenever he moved. When he changed his rooming-house in Philadelphia, in 1944, and neglected to tell the board, Bukowski was arrested by FBI agents and taken to Moyamensing remand prison where he was held until his case was investigated. In the police report, twenty-four year-old Bukowski was described as having 'a florid complexion' so it seems he had been drinking. Bukowski shared a cell with an older inmate named Courtney Taylor whom Bukowski later described as 'public enemy number one'. In fact, Taylor was a relatively harmless con man. The cell-mates gambled together and discussed ways to commit suicide; Bukowski had developed a fixation with killing himself. After fourteen days, he was examined by an army doctor and released.

After his brief imprisonment, Bukowski resumed his writing career. He had a short story published in the avant-garde magazine, *Portfolio*, and contributed stories and poetry to *Matrix*, a small literary magazine in Philadelphia. Even at this early stage, the tone and subject matter of Bukowski's work was distinctive. He wrote about low-life America: characters he met in bars and rooming-houses, and about himself. The pieces were often melancholy, but they were lifted by a sense of humour, like the early short story, 'Love, Love, Love', in which he wrote about being charged rent and board for living at home with his petty-minded father. This was probably the reality of Bukowski's life when he returned to LA in 1947. The relationship between Bukowski and his father was as difficult as ever, so Bukowski soon left to live in a downtown rooming-house. He got a job as a stockman for a department store and spent his evenings drinking in the bars on Alvarado Street, the red-light district bordering MacArthur Park.

He was drinking in a bar one night when he met a diminutive, boss-eyed brunette ten years his senior named Jane Cooney Baker. Jane was from the small town of Roswell, New Mexico, youngest daughter of a family fallen upon hard times. When her army doctor father, Daniel C. Cooney, died young, Jane's widowed mother, Mary, had to go to work to support the family. Jane became a tearaway, scandalising Roswell, and her pious mother, by dating a string of young men, drinking and partying. She became pregnant soon after leaving Roswell High School and hurriedly married Craig Baker, a young man from the nearby town of Artesia. They had two children, but the marriage was not a success. Craig failed in business and began to drink heavily. When he died, apparently in a car accident, shortly after the death of Jane's mother, Jane began to drink excessively and drifted west to California where she lost touch with her family. She lived off the charity of older men, sometimes skivvied in low-rent hotels, and whiled away her spare hours in bars.

Jane allowed Bukowski to drink with her and, according to Bukowski's own account, they went home together that first night. Apart from sex with a prostitute in Philadelphia in 1944, this was the first sexual relationship of Bukowski's life. He was twenty-seven years old. As he wrote, he was so traumatised by his formative experiences that he had become a 'frozen man', unable to make and maintain normal human friendships. Jane was the first person who had got through to him. Characters closely based on Jane appear in his first two novels: she became Betty in *Post Office* and Laura in *Factotum*. He wrote many poems about her, most notably those collected in his 1969 anthology *The Days Run Away Like Wild Horses Over the Hills*. Jane was also the model for Wanda, played by Faye Dunaway in the 1987 motion picture *Barfly*, for which Bukowski wrote the screenplay.

The relationship was marred by jealousy, drunkenness and violence. Jane was flirtatious, and Bukowski was an immature young man who became enraged if he thought Jane was paying attention to other men. They fought so often, and so violently, that they were regularly evicted from the rooms they rented. Bukowski took a job as a temporary mail carrier for the United States Postal Service and would come home from work in the early afternoon. Often, Jane was not there. He sometimes found her drinking with another man, in which case he might slap her before dragging her home. Other times he could not find her, and brooded about what she was doing. Bukowski concluded that Jane was little better than a prostitute, and he came to judge all women against her, commonly referring to women as 'whores'. Another unpleasant legacy of the relationship with Jane is that Bukowski was violent with other women in his life – lashing out when he felt humiliated. In 1971, he punched girlfriend Linda King so hard that he broke her nose.

In the spring of 1955, when Bukowski was living with Jane in small, wood-frame house on North Westmoreland, Bukowski was stricken by a massive internal haemorrhage and was taken by ambulance to the charity ward of Los Angeles County Hospital. Years of heavy drinking had caused a stomach ulcer and it had burst. Ironically, his father saved his life. Because Henry Bukowski had donated blood to the hospital, Bukowski was given a vital blood transfusion. A few days later he was discharged with a warning that he would die if he ever drank again. Bukowski did not feel well enough to go back to work, so he resigned his post office job and convalesced at home. Jane soon left him. At thirty-four years of age, Bukowski was a sickly man with no job, no skills, little education, no money and no girlfriend.

He turned to writing, having had little time or

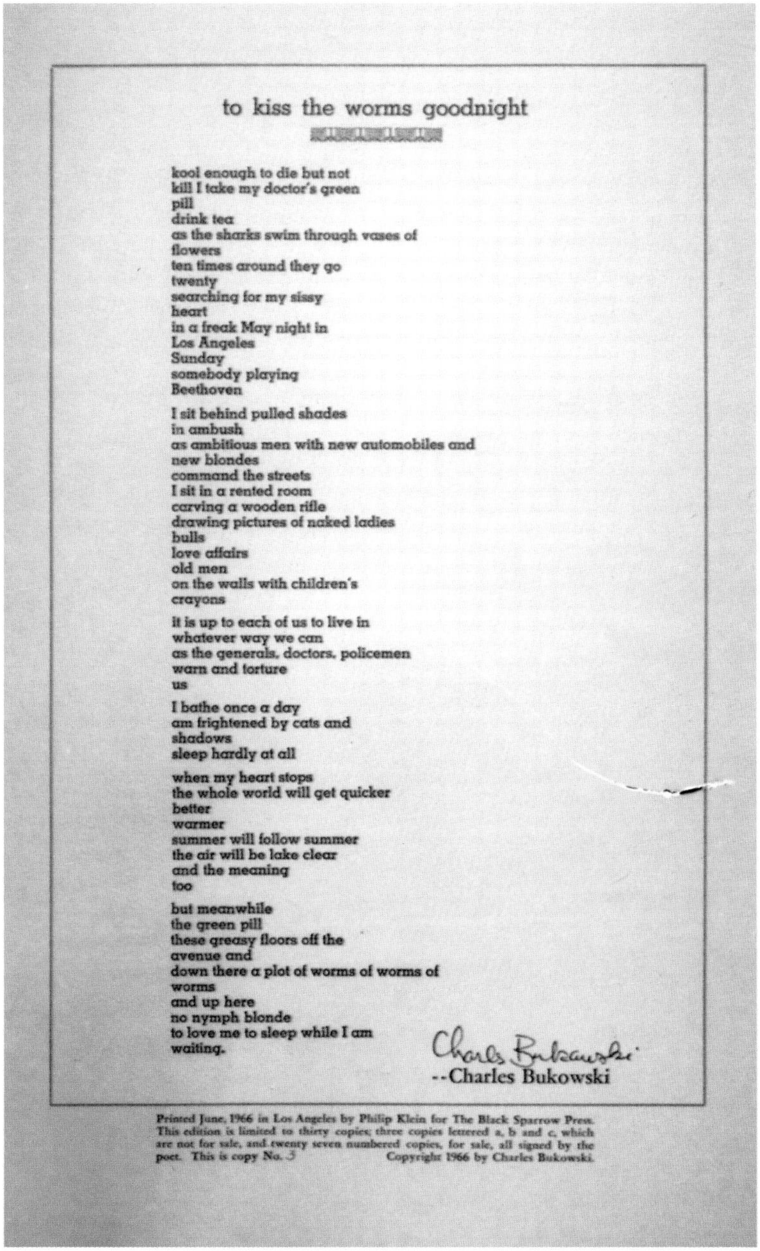

to kiss the worms goodnight

kool enough to die but not
kill I take my doctor's green
pill
drink tea
as the sharks swim through vases of
flowers
ten times around they go
twenty
searching for my sissy
heart
in a freak May night in
Los Angeles
Sunday
somebody playing
Beethoven

I sit behind pulled shades
in ambush
as ambitious men with new automobiles and
new blondes
command the streets
I sit in a rented room
carving a wooden rifle
drawing pictures of naked ladies
bulls
love affairs
old men
on the walls with children's
crayons

it is up to each of us to live in
whatever way we can
as the generals, doctors, policemen
warn and torture
us

I bathe once a day
am frightened by cats and
shadows
sleep hardly at all

when my heart stops
the whole world will get quicker
better
warmer
summer will follow summer
the air will be lake clear
and the meaning
too

but meanwhile
the green pill
these greasy floors off the
avenue and
down there a plot of worms of worms of
worms
and up here
no nymph blonde
to love me to sleep while I am
waiting.

Charles Bukowski
--Charles Bukowski

Printed June, 1966 in Los Angeles by Philip Klein for The Black Sparrow Press.
This edition is limited to thirty copies; three copies lettered a, b and c, which
are not for sale, and twenty seven numbered copies, for sale, all signed by the
poet. This is copy No. 5.   Copyright 1966 by Charles Bukowski.

The poem 'to kiss the worms goodnight' is one of a series of Bukowski poems published by Black Sparrow Press as broadsides in 1966, when businessman John Martin was establishing his publishing company. Each copy was numbered and signed.

(PHOTOGRAPH BY DON KLEIN)

inclination to write when he was with Jane, and began to submit work to small literary magazines. He mostly wrote poetry that dealt with his experiences, but in a more lyrical style than the pared-down verse he later became famous for. The poetry also lacked the power of his later work. Bukowski had considerable difficulty getting anything published. In a desperate letter to small press editor Judson Crews, Bukowski threatened to kill himself if Crews did not publish his poems. Crews sent Bukowski's work straight back, furious he should stoop to emotional blackmail.

When everything seemed hopeless, Bukowski's luck changed. The editor of a literary magazine called *Harlequin* accepted his work for publication. The editor, Barbara Frye, wrote Bukowski an effusive letter saying he was as great a poet as William Blake. Bukowski was delighted and he and Barbara Frye,

Bukowski in the bedroom of his bungalow on Carlton Way, Hollywood, in 1976
(PHOTOGRAPH BY TONY LANE)

who worked as court clerk in Wheeler, Texas, editing *Harlequin* as a hobby, struck up a friendly correspondence. She confided that she had been born with two vertebrae missing from her neck which meant she was unable to turn her head without moving her body. She feared this deformity might prevent her finding a husband. When he was drunk one night, Bukowski wrote back that she should stop worrying. She sounded like a nice girl. If it came to it, he would marry her himself. He thought no more about the letter, but Barbara took him at his word. She quit her job and caught a bus to Los Angeles, writing ahead that she had decided to accept his proposal. When Bukowski met Barbara at the bus terminal downtown, he began to worry. Barbara was very short and did not appear to have any neck. However, Bukowski was not about to turn down an offer of female company. He was a lonely man of thirty-five and Barbara was a young woman of twenty-three who thought he was a genius. The wedding took place on 29 October, 1955.

Barbara, who came from a family of wealthy Texan ranchers, was ambitious for Bukowski. They moved from the shack he had been renting on North Westmoreland to a house in Echo Park. Barbara persuaded Bukowski to go back to Los Angeles City College to obtain qualifications so he could do better than his current employment, which was working as a shipping clerk at an art supply company. Because Bukowski liked to draw and paint, he took a course in commercial art, but soon dropped out. Barbara was disappointed in him and Bukowski began to resent her attempts to improve him. As he wrote in the autobiographical short story, 'Confession of a Coward', he believed his wife saw him as ' ... a goon, a gunnysack, a gutless no-nothing in a world of doers'. Photographs of the couple taken at Christmas, 1956, show an intriguingly ambivalent expression on Bukowski's face. He is trying to be a good husband, putting his arm around his wife as she fondly touches his knee, but the smile on his face is strained. They divorced fifteen months later in March 1958.

It was after Bukowski's divorce that he moved to Hollywood, the district he wrote about so extensively, becoming, along with Raymond Chandler, one of the great chroniclers of the most famous part of Los Angeles County. The first place Bukowski moved to was a rooming-house on North Mariposa, a residential avenue connecting Sunset Boulevard and Hollywood Boulevard. This was the hub of the area Bukowski called East Hollywood, to differentiate it from West Hollywood where the expensive hotels and fashionable restaurants were. East Hollywood was the rag-end of town, dirty streets and poor people, a place of dilapidated rooming-houses, cocktail bars, strip clubs and shabby court motels, everything suffocating under a blanket of sun-baked smog. Bukowski became a regular at the local bars (having disregarded his doctor's advice never to drink again) and a good customer at Ned's liquor store where he shopped for beer, whiskey and cigarettes. He went back to work for the US Postal Service, this time as a mail clerk at the Terminal Annex. He worked night-shifts so he had time during the day to write and go to the horse races, which was a passionate interest. His job was hard. He had to learn complicated schemes and then sort an endless stream of mail against a time-clock. But at least he did not have to talk to people as he had to when he was a mail carrier, delivering door to door. He began seeing Jane again. Their relationship was no longer sexual – alcoholism had aged her and the figure was gone – so they simply drank together.

Bukowski's parents had moved out to the suburb of Temple City, and Bukowski had had little contact with them in recent years. His father complained to neighbours that their son was a drunk who always wanted money. When Bukowski's mother died of cancer, in December 1956, Henry did not bother to inform his son. Two years later Henry died of a heart attack. Henry was buried next to his wife's grave in the Bukowski family plot at the Mountain View cemetery, Altadena, in the foothills of the San Gabriel Mountains. Bukowski celebrated with an orgy of drinking at his parents' bungalow, hosting parties for Jane and neighbours including Francis Billie, who became Harry in the *Notes of a Dirty Old Man* story about the death of Chinaski's father. After selling the house and his father's car, Bukowski inherited approximately fifteen thousand dollars. He claimed he drank and gambled away his inheritance, but the truth is he became careful with money after his parents died and maintained a savings account for most of the rest of his life.

Bukowski did not grieve the death of his parents, but he was not such a cold man that he was unable to experience grief. When Jane Cooney Baker died, Bukowski was devastated.

The tenants of the flea-pit Hollywood hotel where Jane worked as a chambermaid gave her many bottles of liquor for Christmas, 1961. Jane worked her way relentlessly through this stash of booze until she suffered a gastrointestinal haemorrhage. She was taken by ambulance to LA County Hospital and died there on 22 January, 1962, aged fifty-one. Bukowski attended her funeral three days later at the San Fernando Mission, north of Los Angeles, where she was buried in an unmarked grave. It was a miserable end to a tragic life, as he wrote in *Post Office*:

> There was the coffin. What had been Betty was in there. It was very hot. The sun came down in one yellow sheet. A fly circled around. Halfway through the halfway funeral two guys in working clothes came carrying my wreath. The roses were dead, dead and dying in the

heat, and they leaned the thing up against a nearby tree. Near the end of the service my wreath leaned forward and fell flat on its face.

Since the mid-1950s, Bukowski had been writing about working-class people struggling to find happiness in a shabby, unglamorous urban America. As he matured as a man and as an artist he wrote with increasing clarity about his chosen subject matter, usually adding an element of sardonic humour that stopped the work becoming maudlin. After years of practising his craft, after experimenting with different approaches and styles, he began in the early 1960s to produce consistently good writing, achieving what John Martin describes as, 'that … coming together that an artist has to have before he really begins to write publishable work.' Bukowski began to find it slightly easier to get in to print. His work appeared in many small literary magazines and in cheaply produced chapbooks, the first being *Flower, Fist and Bestial Wail* (Hearse Press, 1960). This was followed by *Longshot Pomes* [sic] *for Broke Players* (7 Poets Press, 1962), and *Run With the Hunted* (Midwest Press, 1962). These little books were printed in small editions and sold privately by enthusiastic but amateur poet-publishers.

The Loujon Press, run by Jon and Louise 'Gypsy Lou' Webb, was a cut above Bukowski's previous publishers and an important stepping-stone in his career. The Webbs lived in New Orleans where, despite having almost no money, they launched a high-quality literary magazine, *The Outsider*. Major writers including Allen Ginsberg, Robert Creeley, William Burroughs and Henry Miller featured in the debut issue. Bukowski contributed some of his best early poems including 'Old man, Dead in a room.' In the section of author biographies at the back of the magazine, Jon Webb wrote of Bukowski that he had appeared in ' … more than half a hundred

literary magazines, netting him less than enough $ to spend an evening on the Strip in Los Angeles, where he lives in as much isolation as locked doors & drawn shades in a big city permits', Jon and Gypsy Lou were so impressed by Bukowski's writing that they published a handsome, hand-printed anthology of his best work, *It Catches My Heart in Its Hands* (Loujon Press, 1963). Although this remarkable book reached only a small readership (777 copies were printed, mostly bought by collectors,) it garnered Bukowski more attention than he had previously enjoyed. Two years later the Webbs published a second lavishly produced volume of Bukowski's poetry, *Crucifix in a Deathhand* (Loujon Press, 1965), complete with illustrations by the artist Noel Rockmore. Although the quality of writing was not as strong as the first book, the print run was a little more than three thousand copies and it was a boost for Bukowski's career.

Meanwhile, Bukowski met another woman who became a significant character in his life. Frances Smith, who later changed her name to FrancEyE, was a poet two years older than Bukowski, a divorcee with four daughters by her ex-husband. Her relationship with Bukowski began as a casual friendship, but became more serious when she discovered to her surprise that she was pregnant. At forty-one, she had thought herself too old to have more children. Bukowski was not pleased, having told her he did not want a family. Nevertheless, he asked her to marry him. FrancEyE turned him down, saying she was never going to marry again. They compromised by agreeing to live together. Bukowski left his rented room on North Mariposa and they both went to live in a one-bedroom bungalow on De Longpre Avenue, Hollywood. On 7 September 1964, FrancEyE gave birth to a daughter, Marina Louise. She would be Bukowski's only child and, although his relationship with FrancEyE did not last long, Bukowski was a good father to Marina, keeping in regular contact with his daughter, always paying child support on time and otherwise contributing towards her upbringing. The love he felt for the child was expressed in the poem, 'marina', a poem that shows how tender he could be.

> majestic, magic
> infinite
> my little girl is
> sun
> on the carpet –
> out the door
> picking a
> flower, ha!,
> an old man,
> battle-wrecked,
> emerges from his
> chair
> and she looks at me
> but only sees
> love,
> ha!, and I become
> quick with the world
> and love right back
> just like I was meant
> to do.

Apart from his daughter, and occasional girlfriends, Bukowski was a misanthrope who tried to avoid human company. There were, however, an increasing number of young fans who wanted to meet him, and be his friend. Some managed to strike up an acquaintance with him, although Bukowski was prone to ridicule and abuse them when he was drunk. These friends were mostly young poets, like Neeli Cherkovski, John William Corrington, Steve Richmond and Jory Sherman. They admired Bukowski as an original and authentic poetic voice.

The fact that he lived in an apartment court and worked a factory job made him more appealing, because most of his admirers lived relatively carefree lives. Corrington, for instance, was an academic with a secure teaching job; Steve Richmond lived on the largesse of his wealthy family. Some of these friends, like Blazek and Richmond, published chapbooks of Bukowski work and featured his writing in mimeographed literary magazines. All of this added to Bukowski's reputation.

Despite the support of these friends, and people like Jon and Gypsy Lou Webb, Bukowski was still making virtually no money from his writing and, now in his forties, he felt that it was unlikely he ever would. He seemed doomed to work his factory job until he retired, or it killed him. It was unlikely he would be widely remembered, as he wrote in, 'Old man, Dead in a Room':

> … as my grey hands
> drop a last desperate pen
> in some cheap room
> they will never find me there
> and never know
> my name
> my meaning
> nor the treasure
> of my escape.

His fortunes changed in the spring of 1966. A young businessman, John Martin, came to De Longpre Avenue to tell Bukowski he was a genius poet to rival Walt Whitman, and that he wanted to become his publisher.

It would be hard to envisage a more unlikely pairing than John Martin and Charles Bukowski. Martin is a Christian Scientist and lifelong teetotaller. When he met Bukowski, he was working as the manager of an office supply store. But Martin was not as conventional as he appeared. He was ambitious, single-minded and had a passion for avant-garde writing. Having read Bukowski's early chapbooks, and the two books the Webbs published, he decided to publish Bukowski himself. Using a press at his work, he printed broadsides of five Bukowski poems and won Bukowski's trust by paying him in advance. Martin then sold his collection of first editions and used the capital he raised to start one of the great small publishing houses in America, Black Sparrow Press, the primary purpose of which was to publish Bukowski. John's wife, Barbara Martin, created the sparrow logo and drew the elegant dust jacket designs that make Black Sparrow books so distinctive.

While John Martin was establishing Black

Actor Ben Gazzara starred in the 1981 movie Tales of Ordinary Madness, *which was based on Bukowski's writing. Here the poet is seen meeting Gazzara at a Hollywood motel during filming. Bukowski was not impressed with the finished movie, comparing Gazzara's facial expressions to those of a constipated man.*
(PHOTOGRAPH BY JOE WOLBERG)

Sparrow Press, Bukowski began writing for *Open City*, a radical underground newspaper in Los Angeles. His weekly column, 'Notes of a Dirty Old Man', featured semi-autobiographical short stories. The stories became crude and sexually explicit as he struggled to find material to write about, but the uninhibited nature of these stories appealed strongly to the anti-establishment readers of *Open City*. The wilder the stories became the more they liked them. Bukowski became an unlikely cult figure of the Los Angeles underground scene. This caused problems at work. In January 1968, the US Postal Service was tipped off that Bukowski was writing 'obscene articles' for *Open City*. The informant, probably a fellow worker who had become jealous of Bukowski's notoriety, also told the post office that Bukowski had a child by a woman who was not his wife. This was a situation Bukowski's employers thought might bring the post office into disrepute. On 8 February 1968, after Bukowski clocked on for his night shift, he was called in to see his supervisors. Bukowski confirmed he was the author of the 'Notes of a Dirty Old Man' column and said he had written forty-one articles for *Open City*. His supervisors asked him about specific stories. One was based on the death of Bukowski's father and described a drunken orgy at his father's house with Jane and the man next door. Although not sexually explicit, the story contained crude sexual descriptions. In other stories, Bukowski made references to extremist political groups and ideologies, writing about Adolf Hitler, the Communist Party and the Black Power movement. Asked whether the stories were a true account of his lifestyle and his views, Bukowski said the stories were, 'an inter-mixture of fiction and fact' and that they were, 'highly romanticised in order to give the stories juice'. Asked *why* he wrote such stories, he replied, with poetic spot-on truth, that he wrote them 'for sheer joy'.

Bukowski was asked whether it was true he was

not married to the mother of his child. He admitted it was, but said FrancEyE only shared his apartment 'from time to time for limited periods of a few days'.

Following the interview, Bukowski's supervisors wrote a report concluding that Bukowski's authorship of the *Open City* articles, and the fact he had a child by a woman other than his wife, meant his 'moral character leaves something to be desired'. It might have gone no further than that, but because Bukowski was employed by the post office he was, strictly speaking, an employee of the government. In its officious way, the post office sent Bukowski's report to the Federal Bureau of Investigations in Washington DC, and the FBI decided to launch a full investigation.

The thoroughness with which the FBI investigated Bukowski was absurd considering he was such a lowly employee. It was a nation-wide investigation lasting months. The FBI in Washington researched Bukowski's family history, back to his birth in Andernach, Germany, and the background of his parents. The FBI in Los Angeles contacted Bukowski's former high school and Los Angeles City College – discovering only that he was a mediocre student – and then contacted every company he had worked for in the city, together with every landlord who had rented him a room. Field officers visited these places to interview people who might have some information as to his 'loyalty' to America. The only person they found who had detailed knowledge of Bukowski was his current De Longpre Avenue landlord, Francis Crotty, an avuncular character who stoutly defended Bukowski. However, FBI agents in Philadelphia had discovered that Bukowski had been in prison in the city for failing to keep in touch with the draft board during the war. This information was sent straight to the office of FBI Director J. Edgar Hoover. As Bukowski had failed to declare this arrest, and other arrests for drunkenness, when he applied

for his post office job this might constitute grounds for dismissal.

It did not end there. The FBI made a full investigation of Bukowski's writing career, theorising that, if he wrote for underground magazines, he might be a member of the Communist Party. Apart from asking Bukowski's former employees, neighbours and landlords whether they considered Bukowski a 'loyal American' (those who remembered him thought that he was), field agents in New York, New Orleans, Philadelphia and Los Angeles asked local Communist Party informants whether they knew Bukowski. None of them did. However, the FBI did discover articles by Bukowski had appeared in other radical publications including *Cop Killer*.

While the FBI conducted its investigations in the spring and early summer of 1968, Bukowski was enjoying further success with his writing. His 'Notes of a Dirty Old Man' columns were to be collected as a book of the same name. (It remains one of his most popular books.) Black Sparrow Press was starting to publish anthologies of Bukowski's poetry, and he was making an LP. Bukowski had always taken the maximum amount of sick leave from the post office, but now he was repeatedly absent without leave so he could attend to his writing commitments. It was this absenteeism, rather than the FBI investigation, that led to the final confrontation with the post office. Bukowski was informed by letter in the autumn of 1969 that he was going to be fired for taking too much time off work.

Bukowski put a proposition to his new friend John Martin. In exchange for one hundred dollars a month – enough to cover Bukowski's household bills, living expenses and child support payments for Marina – he would become a full-time writer, giving Black Sparrow Press first refusal on all his work. Martin, who did not know that Bukowski was about to be fired anyway, agreed to the deal. He would pay the money to Bukowski for the rest of his life if he left the post office to write. At the age of forty-nine, Bukowski began what was in many ways a completely new life. As he later wrote in *Post Office*, he felt like a bird escaping from a cage.

The euphoria of leaving the post office was soon replaced with self-doubt and depression. Although Bukowski had loathed his job, resenting the waste of time, and suffering back and shoulder pains because of the repetitive work, it was regular employment with a pension. As a middle-aged man with 'no trade', as he often said, he had little hope of getting another steady job. Despite the safety net of John Martin's hundred dollars a month, he might end up living on the streets, a prospect he dreaded. Bukowski fell so low during the first year after leaving

his job that he considered killing himself. However, there was a steely quality to Bukowski. Despite his drinking, he was not a weak man and he was not lazy. He began to write prolifically, writing himself out of poverty. Within weeks of leaving the post office, Bukowski completed his first novel, *Post Office*, a witty and honest account of his experiences as a delivery man and mail clerk. Bukowski continued to write his newspaper column and he composed reams of poetry. He gave public readings for the first time and began to write for pornographic magazines including *Hustler*.

Although most of his fans were men, Bukowski had a significant following of women readers. Women were intrigued by the honest way he wrote about his feelings, and about sex. However outrageous his stories, Bukowski never spared

Bukowski with girlfriend Linda King.
(PHOTOGRAPH BY JOE WOLBERG)

himself, and his male characters are frequently impotent, alcoholic, unemployed, and grateful for any female company. One of his readers was thirty-year-old sculptress Linda King. After being introduced to Bukowski by a mutual friend, Linda decided she wanted to make a sculpture of him. His large, Germanic head was a fantastic subject – the skin ravaged by acne, nose and cheeks swollen by alcoholism, pig-like eyes and reptilian lips. During the sculpting, Bukowski and Linda became attracted to each other. She resisted at first, considering him too old and too ugly to be a partner. His drinking was also off-putting. 'When I met him, he had just left the post office and [had] taken to drinking with a vengeance,' she explains. 'He was drinking, drinking, drinking. Before he had work, but now he was drinking all day and all night. So when I met him he was in danger of dying, and he was hanging on to me like a life raft.'

Bukowski and Linda King were together almost five years and during that time he became ever more successful. *Post Office* was published to encouraging reviews. His second novel, *Factotum*, was even more warmly received. Black Sparrow Press published several volumes of Bukowski's poetry, including the excellent *Mockingbird Wish Me Luck* (1972) which was dedicated to Linda King, 'for all the good reasons'. The stories Bukowski had been writing for the sex magazines and the underground press were collected and published by Lawrence Ferlinghetti's City Lights Books in a very popular paperback edition, *Erections, Ejaculations, Exhibitions and General Tales of Ordinary Madness* (1972). The book became a cult favourite among college students and its success helped Bukowski become a highly paid reader on college campuses. The fact that he appeared drunk on stage, and frequently insulted his audience, only made him more sought after.

Bukowski began to meet attractive young women who were fascinated by his personality. He took advantage of their attention and had a series of affairs, despite the fact that he was still seeing Linda King. His girlfriends included record company executive, Liza Williams; a rich Texan who wanted to take him to Europe; the former girlfriend of rock star drummer Levon Helm; a series of college girls; and a cocktail waitress named Cupcakes. Linda King was driven to distraction by his infidelities and finally left him in 1975. Their tempestuous relationship became material for the poetry anthology, *Love Is a Dog from Hell* (1977) and his third novel, *Women* (1978).

By the time these two books were finished, Bukowski, was approaching sixty. He began dating Linda Lee Beighle, a restaurateur twenty-three years his junior. Although they frequently argued, Bukowski appreciated the fact that Linda Lee cared for him and wanted to look after him. She worried about his health, trying to get him to eat better food and to drink wine instead of beer and whiskey. She became a friend as much as a lover, and he gradually began to stop seeing his other girlfriends.

Around the same time, Bukowski began to receive the first really substantial royalties from the sale of his books. Surprisingly, the big money was not from America, but from Europe where he had become unexpectedly popular. Books of his short stories and poems sold strongly in France and Italy, but most impressively in Germany where a friend of Bukowski's, Carl Weissner, was a talented and enthusiastic translator of his work. The simplicity of Bukowski's writing, the irreverent wit and the vulgarity – especially in the short stories – appealed to young Germans who were tired of dull post-war German literature. While American editions of his work sold in small print runs of four thousand copies or so, translations of Bukowski in German sold tens of thousands of copies. One anthology known as the

Blue Book (because of the colour of the jacket, rather than the content), sold almost a hundred thousand copies. Bukowski made two trips to Europe in 1978 to help promote his books, the first time he had been outside North America since he was a child. He gave a sold-out reading in Hamburg where the audience listened attentively and respectfully, rather than expecting a drunk show, as audiences in America did. Afterwards, he took the opportunity to visit Andernach, the town of his birth, where his aged Uncle Heinrich Fett (his mother's elder brother) was still alive. Later that year Bukowski went to Paris to appear on the nationally televised arts discussion programme, *Apostrophes*. He became drunk and, after an argument with the host, walked off the show which was being broadcast live. The press coverage ensured that he sold more books than ever.

Bukowski at the race track, with Linda King.
(PHOTOGRAPH BY JOE WOLBERG)

After leaving De Longpre Avenue in 1973, Bukowski settled in an apartment court at 5437 Carlton Way, near the junction of Hollywood Boulevard and Western Avenue – a crossroads meeting place for drug dealers, pimps and prostitutes. Bukowski's neighbours at Carlton Way included a go-go dancer, the manager of a sex shop and a man who worked the door at a massage parlour. It was a dismal, depressing place, one of the worst he had ever lived in, a step backwards. 'Carlton Way was sleazy Hollywood,' says film director Taylor Hackford who made the first television documentary about Bukowski. 'He was taking a stab into his past and almost into his myth. I don't think it was healthy for him. It was a bad scene.' Bukowski's home telephone number was listed in the Hollywood directory and many fans would call him up, wanting to meet the famous 'Dirty Old Man'. The fans would bring beer and drugs over to his apartment on Carlton Way, wanting to get stoned with Bukowski, and women would visit just to say they had had sex with him. It became a debauched and sometimes undignified situation, with Bukowski acting up to his image and his visitors taking advantage of him in any way they could, including stealing books and magazines from the collection he kept of his published work.

Bukowski did not stay long. As soon as he saved enough money to make a down payment, he bought a detached house in the suburb of San Pedro, the port town south of Los Angeles. Within a few years he was wealthy enough to pay off the mortgage. He then exchanged his old Volkswagen for a smart new BMW. After a lifetime of near-poverty, after working in factories, or barely working at all, Bukowski had no compunction about enjoying his success. He derived enormous pleasure from his new car, his new home and his money. He had a small swimming pool installed in the garden. He ate at good restaurants, including The Musso & Frank Grill in Hollywood;

he drank expensive wine, and he had the BMW valet-parked when he went to the horse races. In 1985 he married for the second time, to Linda Lee. They were driven to the ceremony in a Rolls Royce. Bukowski now had it all – the home, the car, money in the bank and a young wife to look after him. He did not become complacent, however. He continued to write prolifically, composing poetry that described the change in his fortunes, while insisting that his essential values remained the same. Black Sparrow Press published this work in books including *War All the Time* (1984) and *You Get So Alone at Times That It Just Makes Sense* (1986). He also wrote a powerful fourth novel, *Ham on Rye* (1982), based on his unhappy childhood.

Shortly after the move to San Pedro, Bukowski was contacted by a film director, Barbet Schroeder, who wanted to make a motion picture based on Bukowski's stories. Bukowski agreed to write an original screenplay and this became the basis of the movie *Barfly*. Getting the film made was a tedious process, but Bukowski got to meet some of the most famous names in Hollywood as Schroeder cast the film. He met Harry Dean Stanton, Elliott Gould, James Woods, Dennis Hopper and Sean Penn, who became a close friend. Sean Penn, like other Hollywood stars, admired Bukowski as an artist who did not compromise his work. Bukowski and Linda Lee went out for dinner with Penn and his then wife, Madonna, and Penn was a regular visitor at the house at San Pedro. Bukowski became so fond of his actor friend that he dedicated a book to him, *In the Shadow of the Rose* (1991). After Bukowski's death, Penn returned the compliment by dedicating his 1996 film, *The Crossing Guard*, to Bukowski.

Mickey Rourke eventually accepted the lead in *Barfly*, playing Henry Chinaski. Faye Dunaway took the female lead as Wanda, a character based on Jane Cooney Baker. The film, which was made in 1987,

was not entirely convincing. Bukowski had no experience of screenwriting and failed to provide the film with sufficient narrative drive. Curiously, the screenplay also lacked Bukowski's sense of humour. The film was not a commercial success, but it raised Bukowski's profile in America where sales of his books still lagged behind Europe.

For Christmas 1990, Linda Lee gave Bukowski an Apple Macintosh computer and Bukowski's use of this machine had a marked effect on his writing. He had always been a prolific writer. Now he wrote with renewed energy. Bukowski's spelling was poor and, previously, his habit had been to write at night on a typewriter, while drinking and listening to classical music on the radio. The following night he would hand-correct his mistakes. Finally, he typed a clean copy to send to John Martin. It was a laborious process, and he still made mistakes of spelling and punctuation that embarrassed him. He was delighted by the almost magical way the Apple Mac corrected his spelling, and he also found the innovations of editing text a marvellous aid to creativity. Bukowski composed thousands of new poems every year on the Apple Mac, work John Martin edited into big poetry anthologies like *The Last Night of the Earth Poems* (1992) which runs to 405 pages. It is one of Bukowski's great collections. Looking back over his entire life, and using a simple anecdotal style of blank verse, he reviewed his childhood, his years of obscurity, the factory jobs, his relationships and his late, unexpected success. The poems were often surprisingly tender, revealing the sensitive soul behind the hard-man image. He expressed this sensitivity most eloquently in his poem, 'the bluebird':

there's a bluebird in my heart that
wants to get out
but I'm too tough for him,

I say, stay in there, I'm not going
to let anybody see
you.

… he's singing a little
in there, I haven't quite let him
die
and we sleep together like
that
with our
secret pact
and it's nice enough to

make a man
weep, but I don't
weep, do
you?

Bukowski continued to write short stories, and some of his best appeared in *Septuagenarian Stew* (1990), the book published to celebrate his seventieth birthday. He also wrote a fourth novel, *Hollywood* (1989), a good-natured *roman-a-clef* based on his experiences in the movie industry. In the book, Henry Chinaski finds the absurd antics of desperate film producers

Bukowski at the Hollywood Park race track with Linda Lee Beighle.
(PHOTOGRAPH BY JOE WOLBERG)

and spoilt movie actors crazier and more bizarre than his own youthful experiences:

> Back at the house I went upstairs and did work on the screenplay but strangely or maybe not so strangely my past life hardly seemed as strange or wild or as mad as what was occurring now.

By the early 1990s, with more than twenty books in print, Bukowski was making in excess of one hundred thousand dollars a year. The life of the former post office clerk had been transformed beyond recognition. He was also as happy as he had ever been. Then, when everything seemed near perfect, Bukowski became seriously ill.

Following the completion of his novel, *Hollywood*, he contracted tuberculosis. A course of antibiotics was prescribed. The medication would not work if he drank, so Bukowski had to learn to live without alcohol. He eventually conquered the tuberculosis, but this was only the start of his troubles. Other unpleasant and irritating ailments included a cataract that had to be operated on. Then he discovered he had leukaemia. For much of 1993 Bukowski was an in-patient at San Pedro Peninsula Hospital where he endured chemotherapy treatment with great dignity. When he was in remission, he went home and put the finishing touches to his sixth novel, *Pulp*, a curious detective story unlike anything he had written. Marina came to stay and Bukowski was visited regularly by a hospital doctor who had become a friend. He saw few other people. When he had the energy, he sent John Martin short notes and faxes that showed him to be bravely making the best of his worsening condition.

In March 1994, Bukowski developed pneumonia and had to go back into hospital. The doctors cured the pneumonia, but his body was so weakened by chemotherapy that the doctors struggled to keep him alive. Linda Lee and Marina were with when he died on the morning of Wednesday 9 March, 1994. He was seventy-three.

In the years since Bukowski's death his reputation has continued to grow. He is now as popular in the United States of America as he is in Europe, and all his books are available in more than a dozen languages, making him one of the most widely read modern poets. Bukowski's visionary publisher John Martin has helped keep Bukowski's flame alight by editing and publishing new collections of Bukowski's work, including the 1999 edition, *What Matters Most Is How Well You Walk Through the Fire*. The final poem in the book is 'roll the dice'. Simple and direct, like the best of Bukowski's poetry, it is the voice of a wise and courageous man who was not defeated by personal or professional setbacks. He forged through adversity, taking joy from his talent, and leaving words to inspire.

if you're going to try,
go all the way.
there is no other feeling like
that.
you will be alone with the
gods
and the nights will flame with
fire.

do it, do it, do it.
do it.

all the way.
all the way.

you will ride life straight to
perfect laughter, it's
the only good fight
there is.

In his darker moments Bukowski's philosophy was bleak indeed. Life was a horror show. His fellow human beings cavorted through the streets of Los Angeles as if they would live forever, accumulating money, buying bigger homes, scrabbling their way to better jobs. It was a pitiful joke to Bukowski. These people were already dead in their souls and would soon be actually underground. Their frantic activity was like the jiggling dance of the ghouls in Saint-Saëns' symphonic poem *Danse Macabre*.

His attitude was that people brought bad luck and hurt. Misanthropy was born out of his relationship with his father Henry, who beat him as a child, and it was there throughout his life.

Bukowski could not escape people, of course. In everyday life – the graveyard above the ground, as he once called it – he was forced to be with them. Poverty meant he had to live in cramped apartment courts. The need for money made him drag his bones to work. The need to get drunk led him into bars.

In his mind, he was haunted by people from his past. Bukowski could never shake memories of his cruel father. He also thought about his mother, and why she had not intervened to help him. His paternal grandparents had left a strong impression. The old man, Leonard, was a veteran of the German army. A heavy drinker, he separated from Bukowski's grandmother, Emilie. Their children – Bukowski's uncles and aunts – were quarrelsome. Henry Bukowski said spiteful things to his siblings, even when his brother Ben was dying in a sanatorium. It seemed the whole Bukowski family was angry at life.

In *Ham on Rye*, his novel of childhood, Bukowski wrote:

The first thing I remember my grandmother saying was, 'I will bury *all* of you!' She said this the first time just before we began eating a meal, and she was to say it many times after

that, just before we began to eat. Eating seemed very important. We ate mashed potatoes and gravy, especially on Sundays. We also ate roast beef, knockwurst and sauerkraut, green peas, rhubarb, carrots, spinach, string beans, chicken, meatballs and spaghetti, sometimes mixed with ravioli; there were boiled onions, asparagus, and every Sunday there was strawberry shortcake with vanilla ice cream. For breakfasts we had French toast and sausages, or there were hotcakes or waffles with bacon and scrambled eggs on the side. And there was always coffee. But what I remember best is all the mashed potatoes and gravy and my grandmother, Emily [*sic*], saying, 'I will bury *all* of you!

Surviving family photographs show the 'battling Bukowskis', as Bukowski's cousin Katherine Wood calls them. Stiff-backed, unsmiling, Germanic people, seemingly unable to derive any joy from life, they are the inspiration for characters in books like *Ham on Rye*, the genetic stock from which Bukowski came, sepia-tinted ghosts he was never able to shake.

THIS GRAVEYARD ABOVE THE GROUND

Bukowski's father, Henry, wanted to be an engineer but could only find work as a milkman. Thwarted ambition made him resentful and he became a charmless and boorish snob of a man who was also sadistically cruel to his wife and son. He is seen here in the mid-1920s standing next to an orange grove in his home town of Pasadena, California. In Ham on Rye, *Bukowski wrote about his father trying to steal oranges from an orange grove and being seen off by the irate farmer.*
(PHOTOGRAPH COURTESY OF KARL FETT)

RIGHT

This is the house in Andernach, Germany, where Charles Bukowski was born on 16 August 1920. The building later became the town brothel.

(PHOTOGRAPH BY HOWARD SOUNES)

BELOW RIGHT

The infant Bukowski was baptized in this medieval font at the Mariendom, Andernach's cathedral. The iron bird on the lid of the font looks very much like the black sparrow later used by John and Barbara Martin as the logo for Black Sparrow Press.

(FROM THE COLLECTION OF HOWARD SOUNES)

BELOW

Bukowski and his parents sailed from Bremerhaven, Germany, to the United States on 18 April, 1923. This post card is the one Kate Bukowski sent to her parents before they embarked. It shows the ship upon which they travelled.

(COURTESY OF KARL FETT)

UNITED STATES LINES S.S. PRESIDENT FILLMORE U.S. GOVERNMENT SHIP

DUPLICATE

(Form No. 216—Consular.)

CONSULT GENERAL INSTRUCTION NO. 652 WHEN EXECUTING THIS FORM.

REPORT OF BIRTH
OF CHILDREN BORN TO AMERICAN PARENTS.
AMERICAN CONSULAR SERVICE.

Coblens, Germany, March 8, 1922

Name of child in full... Henry Charles BUKOWSKI... Sex... Mabe.

Date of birth... August 16 1920 10 a.m.

Place of birth... Room Strasse 12, Andernach, Germany.

Father:

Full name... Henry Charles BUKOWSKI... Age 29

Occupation... Contracting business.

Present residence... Pfaffendorf, Hoch Strasse 40, Germany.

Birthplace... Pasedena, Cal.

Naturalized (if foreign born)... Native born.

Registered as American citizen... No.

Passport... x x x x

Mother:

Full name... Katharina Fett BUKOWSKI... Age 26

Name before marriage... Katharina Fett

Present residence... Hoch Strasse 40, Pfaffendorf, Germany.

Birthplace... Neisoenturm, Germany.

Naturalized (if foreign born)... through marriage with Henry Charles Bukowski, certificate # 56, Andernach, Ger.

Registered as American citizen... No.

Passport... x x x x

Number of previous children... None. Number now living... One.

Physician or nurse... Frau Ludwig, Hoch Strasse, Andernach, Germany.

(Signature of parent, physician, or nurse.)

German Empire
Rheinprovince ss:
Coblens

Subscribed and sworn to before me at Coblens, Germany,
this 8th day of March, 1922.

ABOVE

Bukowski was born in Germany to an American serviceman so his birth had to be registered with the American Consular Service. This is the certificate.

(FROM THE COLLECTION OF HOWARD SOUNES)

This photograph, taken in Andernach, Germany, shows Bukowski's maternal grandparents. Nanatte and Wilhelm Fett are the couple seated in front. There is a strong facial resemblance between Bukowski and his grandfather.

(COURTESY OF KARL FETT)

MAIN PICTURE
After Henry Bukowski settled his family in Los Angeles, and got a job as a milkman, he bought this Model-T Ford and would take the family on weekend excursions. Here Kate Bukowski poses for her picture.
(COURTESY OF KARL FETT)

TOP RIGHT
Bukowski and his parents moved several times when they first came to live in Los Angeles in the 1920s. This Spanish-style house at 4511 S. 28th Street was one of their homes. Bukowski attended Virginia Road Elementary School two blocks away.
(PHOTOGRAPH BY HOWARD SOUNES)

BOTTOM RIGHT
These two photographs show Bukowski's parents on a day out at Santa Monica Beach, California. The Santa Monica pier with its funfair can be seen in the background.
(COURTESY OF KARL FETT)

24

ABOVE

*Bukowski's father, Henry Bukowski,
was raised as one of six children in
Pasadena, California. His father,
Leonard, was a successful builder.
This is the comfortable home he built
for his family.*

(COURTESY OF KATHERINE WOOD)

RIGHT

*Bukowski's paternal grandparents,
Emilie and Leonard Bukowski. Emilie
was a formidable woman who became
very religious in later life. She
separated from Leonard Bukowski
who had a taste for liquor.*

(COURTESY OF KATHERINE WOOD)

FACING PAGE, TOP

*Emilie Bukowski (left) favoured
Bukowski's mother Kate (seen on the
right) over other relations because of
her old-fashioned German manners.
Kate sent this photograph home to
Germany saying of her mother in law,
'She loves me very much.'*

(COURTESY OF KARL FETT)

FACING PAGE, BOTTOM

*The infant Bukowski sits on his
father's knee in Pasadena, California.*

(COURTESY OF KARL FETT)

26

Mother & Father

LEFT

John Bukowski was Henry's eldest brother and is seen here in army uniform during World War I. Bukowski later wrote about John in his novel Ham on Rye, *saying he was a ne'er-do-well and drunk. In a poem entitled 'the bones of my uncle' Bukowski implied that John Bukowski had been in trouble with the police, for a fraud and a sexual offence:*

the bones of my uncle
rode a motorcycle in Arcadia *
and raped a housewife
within a garage
hung with rakes and hoses
the bones of my Uncle
left behind
1: a jar of peanut butter
and
2: two girls named
Katherine &
Betsy and
3: a ragged wife who cried
continually.

…

I almost forgot to tell you:
his bones were named 'John'
and
had green eyes
which did not
last.

There is no evidence that John – who died in 1933 – did commit these crimes, and his surviving daughter, Katherine, dismisses the allegations. 'It made me furious,' she says, of the poem. 'I think the booze was just talking. The man [Bukowski] was a drunk.'
(PHOTOGRAPH COURTESY OF KATHERINE WOOD)
* *Arcadia is a suburban town near Pasadena*

After the family moved to 2122 Longwood Avenue in 1931, Bukowski's father began to beat him with sadistic regularity. These punishments were triggered by petty matters – like not cutting the grass properly – and would be inflicted in the bathroom with a leather razor strop. Kate Bukowski would stand impassively by during the punishments.

Bukowski was discouraged from talking or playing at home, his father firmly believing in the maxim that children should be seen and not heard. His father also tried to stop Bukowski mixing with neighbourhood children, snobbishly believing that the Bukowskis were better than their neighbours. As Bukowski wrote in *Ham on Rye*, it wasn't long before he hated his father. But at first he suppressed his anger, being too young to do anything about it.

Bukowski believed that the acne that erupted when he entered adolescence was a physical manifestation of the misery pent up inside him. It was an extraordinarily unpleasant case of acne, covering his face, chest, back and shoulders in huge boils so disfiguring that he had to go to hospital to have them lanced with an electric drill. He wrote about these treatments in his short story, *Confessions of a Man Insane Enough to Live With Beasts:*

> It was like a wood drill, it might have been a wood drill, I could smell the oil burning, and they'd stick that thing into my head into my flesh and it would drill and bring up blood and puss, and I'd sit there the monkey of my soul-string dangling over the edge of a cliff. I was covered with boils the size of small apples. It was ridiculous and unbelievable. Worst case I ever saw, said one of the docs, and he was old. They'd gather around me like some freak. I was a freak. I'm still a freak. I rode the streetcar back and forth to the charity ward. Children on streetcars would stare and ask their mothers, 'What's wrong with that man? Mother, what's wrong with that man's *face?*' And the mother would SHUUSSSHHH!!! That shuussshhh was the worst condemnation, and then they'd continue to let the little bastards and bastardesses stare from over the backs of their seats and I'd look out the window and watch the buildings go by, and I'd be drowning, slugged and drowning, nothing to do. The doctors for lack of anything else called it Acne Vulgaris.

The acne made an already shy and withdrawn child a freak at school. Bukowski enrolled at Los Angeles High School in 1937, joining a student body of apparently happy, well-adjusted young people from affluent and congenial homes. They all appeared attractive and confident to Bukowski, who crept about, too timid to speak to anybody but a few friends, unable to make any contact with girls, feeling like the Hunchback of Notre Dame. He was so ashamed of his appearance that he opted out of gym class because he did not want other boys to see the boils on his shoulders. Instead, he paraded as a pretend soldier in the uniform of the Reserve Officers' Training Corps.

While Bukowski endured these miserable years at LA High the school was used, with supreme irony, as the set for a breezy Jackie Cooper comedy entitled *What a Life.*

WHAT A LIFE

2122 Longwood Avenue, Los Angeles – the bungalow home that Bukowski and his parents moved to in 1931 and where he spent his teenage years. The lawn in front is the lawn Bukowski's father made him manicure every weekend. If a single blade of grass was left standing after the job was done, the boy was taken back into the bathroom and beaten.

(COURTESY OF KARL FETT)

LOS ANGELES HIGH SCHOOL · FOUNDED · 1873 · ROMANS

ABOVE

Bukowski joined the Reserve Officers' Training Corps at school rather than expose his body to fellow pupils in gym class. He can be seen on the top row of this series of photographs, fourth from the left.

(FROM THE COLLECTION OF HOWARD SOUNES)

LEFT

James Haddox was one of Bukowski's few friends at LA High School. He was used as the basis of the character of Jimmy in Ham on Rye.

(FROM THE COLLECTION OF HOWARD SOUNES)

NEXT PAGES

Members of the Reserve Officers' Training Corps (ROTC) practice drill on the field of Los Angeles High School in the late 1930s. Charles Bukowski was a member of ROTC and won a medal for his drill. But the real reason he joined ROTC was because it meant he did not have to take part in gym class and fellow pupils would not see the acne on his shoulders and back. The ROTC uniform covered up his disfigured body.

(FROM THE COLLECTION OF HOWARD SOUNES)

The grand façade of LA High School, which Bukowski attended from 1937 until his graduation in 1939.

(FROM THE COLLECTION OF HOWARD SOUNES)

LEFT

In 1939 Bukowski graduated from LA High School. The graduation was described in his novel Ham on Rye *and this photograph was used for the cover of the original Black Sparrow Press edition of the novel.*

(FROM THE COLLECTION OF HOWARD SOUNES)

BOTTOM

This is the commencement booklet for Bukowski's graduation ceremony in the summer of 1939, showing lyrics to the stirring school song, 'Hail! Hail! LA High!'

(FROM THE COLLECTION OF HOWARD SOUNES)

After school Bukowski briefly attended Los Angeles City College, dropping out in 1941. He then left home and went to live in downtown Los Angeles. Here at the Los Angeles Public Library he discovered John Fante's novel *Ask the Dust*. This strongly autobiographical novel – written in a simple and compelling style – had an enormous influence on Bukowski's life and career. Years later he expressed his debt to Fante in a preface to a new Black Sparrow Press edition of the book (published in the United Kingdom by Rebel Inc).

Bukowski began by explaining his situation before he first discovered the book:

I was a young man, starving and drinking and trying to be a writer. I did most of my reading at the downtown LA Public Library, and nothing that I read related to me or to the streets or to the people about me. It seemed as if everybody was playing word-tricks, that those who said almost nothing at all were considered excellent writers.

Then he found *Ask the Dust* …

… like a man who had found gold in the city dump, I carried the book to a table. The lines rolled easily across the page, there was a flow. Each line had its own energy and was followed by another like it. The very substance of each line gave the page a form, a feeling of something *carved* into it. And here, at last, was a man who was not afraid of emotion. The humour and the pain were intermixed with a superb simplicity. The beginning of that book was a wild and enormous miracle to me.

He was excited to be living in downtown LA, the place where Fante set his novel. After a while he decided to set out across America in search of experiences that would allow him to turn his own life into a Fante-style story. In this way he embarked on what has become known as his 'lost years' – a period of time beginning in 1941 and ending in the early 1950s. Living in cheap rooming-houses, working manual jobs and drinking in bars, he collected the primal experiences that became basic material for his writing.

He went without work as much as possible so he was able to stay in his room and write. But apart from limited success with small literary magazines in New York and Philadelphia, his submissions were rejected by publishers. Half starved and driven nearly mad with loneliness he seriously contemplated killing himself. As a young man of age to be called up for military service during World War II, he also found himself imprisoned briefly when he failed to keep in contact with the army draft board.

Yet drunkenness, starvation and imprisonment was not the complete story of Bukowski's lost years. Bukowski would occasionally return to his parents' house in Los Angeles. The photograph on the opposite page was taken during one of these visits, in 1947. Caught between his thwarted ambition to be a writer, and his parents' desire for him to pursue a regular career, he is seen dressed for what might well have been a job interview. This photograph does not lesson the validity of Bukowski's experiences, but it does illustrate a paradox in his personality: Bukowski was a wild man plunging the depths of human experience, but he was also a practical and industrious man. Even in his darkest hours, he maintained a roof over his head and had money in his pocket.

Not quite the hobo poet of legend, Bukowski appears neatly dressed in suit and tie in July 1947, in the middle of the ten year period he claimed to have spent as an itinerant drunk.

(COURTESY OF KARL FETT)

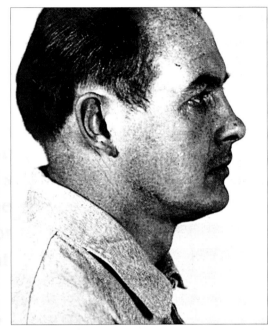

FACING PAGE
Bukowski lived in Philadelphia, Pennsylvania, in the early 1940s. He made his home in run-down tenement buildings and rooming-houses in inner city neighbourhoods including the Spring Garden District. The movie Barfly *was partly based on his experiences here. This photograph, taken in 1941, shows one of the dilapidated tenements in the Spring Garden neighbourhood.*
(COURTESY OF THE URBAN ARCHIVES, TEMPLE UNIVERSITY, PHILADELPHIA)

LEFT
Bukowski was of age in the mid-1940s to be called up for military service. When he failed to keep in touch with the draft board he was arrested by the FBI *and briefly held in Moyamensing prison, Philadelphia. This is a unique photograph of Bukowski's cell mate, Courtney Taylor, a fraudster who appears as a character in several of Bukowski's poems and stories, invariably described as 'public enemy number one'.*
(COURTESY OF THE URBAN ARCHIVES, TEMPLE UNIVERSITY, PHILADELPHIA)

FAR LEFT AND BELOW
Moyamensing Prison as it was around the time Bukowski was imprisoned here for failing to keep in contact with the army draft board.
(COURTESY OF THE URBAN ARCHIVES, TEMPLE UNIVERSITY, PHILADELPHIA)

BACKGROUND
Aftermath of a Lengthy Rejection Slip *was the first piece of writing Bukowski ever had published. A humorous account of Bukowski's own struggle to become a writer, it appeared in the literary magazine,* Story, *in the spring of 1944.*
(FROM THE COLLECTION OF HOWARD SOUNES)

MAIN PICTURE AND INSETS
Tall stone-clad buildings with iron fire escapes give downtown Los Angeles a claustrophobic atmosphere very different to the rest of LA and more typical of cities like New York. These are scenes of downtown LA that would have been familiar to Bukowski when he lived here in 1940-41.

TOP LEFT
The entrance to the Los Angeles Public Library on West 5th Street, where Bukowski discovered Ask the Dust.

BOTTOM LEFT
Angels Flight, the funicular railway Bukowski would have taken to the top of Bunker Hill. This was the district of downtown LA that Fante wrote about in Ask the Dust, *and where Bukowski himself lived.*

(PHOTOGRAPHS BY HOWARD SOUNES)

41

The tragic figure of Jane Cooney Baker casts a long shadow over Bukowski's life and work. She was the inspiration for the character of Betty in *Post Office*, Laura in *Factotum* and Wanda in *Barfly*.

Jane's father, Daniel C. Cooney, died when she was a child and she was raised by her mother, Mary, in Roswell, New Mexico, where she gained a reputation for fast living. She became pregnant almost directly upon leaving school, and in 1928 she hastily married a young man named Craig Baker. Her husband was a heavy drinker and died young, leaving her with two children. Jane seems to have blamed herself for his death and consoled herself with drink. She moved to California, lost touch with her family, and became a 'barfly' – someone who spends their time hanging around bars. It was here that Bukowski met her in the mid-1940s.

They began a love affair that was hugely important to Bukowski because it was his first. Alcoholism and jealousy meant it was a turbulent relationship. They eventually separated in 1954, but maintained a friendship.

During the separation, Bukowski married and divorced. His first wife was a poetess and small press publisher from Texas named Barbara Frye. She had a deformity of the neck which meant she could not move her head without moving her body. They married on 29 October 1955 and divorced, after Barbara suffered a miscarriage, two and a half years later.

Bukowski's mother died of cancer in 1956. His father died in 1958, leaving an inheritance of approximately $15,000. Jane Cooney Baker was around to help Bukowski celebrate the death of his hated father with a wild drinking spree.

Jane was working as a maid in a small hotel in Hollywood when she died in 1962, aged fifty-one. The primary cause of death was cancer, but she also had cirrhosis of the liver. Her funeral was a pitiful affair. Hardly any mourners attended and she was buried in an unmarked grave.

The tragic circumstances of Jane's death moved Bukowski to write some of his most powerful early poetry. The poem 'for Jane' shows how deeply he felt her loss:

225 days under grass
and you know more than I.

they have long taken your blood,
you are a dry stick in a basket.

is this how it works?

in this room
the hours of love
still make shadows.

when you left
you took almost
everything.

I kneel in the nights
before tigers
that will not let me be.

JANE, WITH ALL THE LOVE I HAD WHICH WAS NOT ENOUGH

Jane Cooney Baker was the great love of Bukowski's early life. This high school picture – taken when she was seventeen – is the only photograph of Jane to have been discovered.

(COURTESY OF ROSWELL HIGH SCHOOL)

ABOVE

The entrance to the room Bukowski shared with Jane Cooney Baker at an apartment court at 268 S. Coronado Street, Los Angeles.

(PHOTOGRAPH BY HOWARD SOUNES)

RIGHT

Afternoon sunlight streams into the S. Coronado Street apartment court where Bukowski and Jane lived from 1951-1952.

(PHOTOGRAPH BY HOWARD SOUNES)

FACING PAGE

In 1954 Bukowski and Jane Cooney Baker briefly lived at the Aragon apartment house on South WestLake Avenue, Los Angeles. Bukowski and Jane were evicted from the building. The inserted 'Notice to Quit' shows they were thrown out for 'excessive drinking, fighting and foul language …' The notice is addressed to Mr and Mrs Bukowski because Bukowski and Jane had to pose as a married couple to get rented rooms. They never actually married. This building was later used as a set for the movie Barfly.

(PHOTOGRAPH OF BUILDING BY HOWARD SOUNES/ EVICTION NOTICE FROM THE COLLECTION OF HOWARD SOUNES)

THIS PAGE

In the mid 1950s, Bukowski worked various manual jobs including a job as a shipping clerk at the Graphic Arts Center on West 7th Street in Los Angeles. He liked this job partly because it was within walking distance of two favourite bars – Vince & Paul's (top) and The Seven Gs (bottom).

(PHOTOGRAPHS BY HOWARD SOUNES)

FACING PAGE

In the spring of 1955 Bukowski suffered a massive internal haemorrhage, caused by excessive drinking. Because he didn't have medical insurance, he was brought to the charity ward of this austere building, the Los Angeles County Hospital. It is the same place he was treated as a teenager for his acne. His life was saved by a blood transfusion and doctors warned him he must never drink again. It was advice he ignored.

(PHOTOGRAPH BY HOWARD SOUNES)

48

LEFT

Barbara Frye became Bukowski's first wife in October 1955. A small press publisher from Wheeler, Texas, she had a physical deformity that made her appear to be hunching her shoulders. Bukowski would write about her extensively in his novel Post Office, *where she becomes Joyce, and in* Notes of a Dirty Old Man *where he used her real name.*

(COURTESY OF LEAH BELLE WILSON)

BELOW

Barbara Frye published Bukowski's work in her small literary magazine, Harlequin. *For some reason she chose to spell her name 'Fry' on the cover.*

(FROM THE COLLECTION OF HOWARD SOUNES)

Vol. II   No. 1

HARLEQUIN

FICTION

bukowski

ARTICLE

snook

POETRY

bukowski
fielder
eigner
garrett
johnson
kaplan
millett
pettinella
schoeberlein
turco

FEATURE

may

EDITORS: Barbara Fry — W. R. Lasater

HARLEQUINS: P.O. Box 75-451, Sanford Station, Los Angeles 5, California. Irregular. $1.00 per copy. Manuscripts returned only when accompanied by self-addressed, stamped envelopes............
Copyright, 1957, by Barbara Fry

ABOVE

This is a copy of the marriage certificate of
Charles Bukowski and Barbara Frye. They
married in Nevada.

(FROM THE COLLECTION OF HOWARD SOUNES)

ABOVE LEFT

This photo of Barbara Frye was taken in Texas
a year before her marriage to Bukowski.

(COURTESY OF LEAH BELLE WILSON)

LEFT

This is one of only two pictures of Bukowski
and his first wife to have been discovered. It was
taken in December 1956.

(COURTESY OF LEAH BELLE WILSON)

RIGHT

When Bukowski's father died, Bukowski inherited his house in the Los Angeles suburb of Temple City. During the settlement of the estate Bukowski and Jane stayed at the house and would drink with neighbour Francis Billie, an ornithologist with a collection of rare birds. Bukowski wrote an outrageous short story based on his evenings with Mr Billie – whom he called Harry in the story – later published in Notes of a Dirty Old Man.

Francis Billie had got to know Henry Bukowski quite well, and would listen to him talk about his son. 'He was disappointed in his son. The son always wanted money,' he said. 'He said … his son drank too much.'

(PHOTOGRAPH BY HOWARD SOUNES)

LEFT

This is the house at Doreen Avenue, Temple City, that Bukowski inherited after his father died in 1958. It is the house he wrote about in Notes of a Dirty Old Man, *in the story about the death of his father. After the estate was settled Bukowski received approximately $15,000.*

(PHOTOGRAPH BY HOWARD SOUNES)

ABOVE

In the last years of her life Jane Cooney Baker worked as a maid in the this hotel, the Phillips, on Vermont Avenue, Hollywood. She died two days after suffering a haemorrhage here on 20 January, 1962. The death was described vividly in Post Office.

(PHOTOGRAPH BY HOWARD SOUNES)

MAIN PICTURE

Jane was buried following a sad little funeral, here at the San Fernando Mission, north of Los Angeles, on 25 January 1962. Few people attended and her grave – seen here in the foreground between the two grey tablets – remains unmarked. Again the funeral was described by Bukowski in Post Office.

(PHOTOGRAPH BY HOWARD SOUNES)

54

ABOVE

Jane Cooney Baker's death certificate shows her body was rotten with cancer and cirrhosis when she died.

(FROM THE COLLECTION OF HOWARD SOUNES)

After his divorce from Barbara Frye in 1958, Bukowski moved to Hollywood, the district of Los Angeles that would be his home until 1978. In that period of twenty years Bukowski went from being a post office clerk to a writer of distinction, and much of what he wrote was inspired by his surroundings.

For the first six years he lived in a rented apartment at 1623 North Mariposa Avenue. The building was an old Spanish-style rooming-house with twenty-four tiny rooms arranged like prison cells along narrow corridors. Bukowski took room 303 on the second floor. It was a cold water apartment with no air conditioning. The bathroom was shared. At night he had to pull a retractable Murphy bed out from the wall. Visitors remember room 303 as the quintessence of seediness – broken down sticks of furniture, dirty crockery in the sink and a gaping crack in the wall. Bukowski patched the peeling wallpaper together with pieces of sticky tape.

North Mariposa Avenue is sandwiched between two of the most famous thoroughfares in Hollywood – Hollywood Boulevard and Sunset Boulevard – place names synonymous with glamour. From his window Bukowski had a fine view of the gleaming white dome of the Griffith Observatory in the Hollywood Hills. Clustered around the observatory were the homes of movie actors, directors, artists and writers including Aldous Huxley. But to look up at the lights of houses in the Hills was to be in the gutter looking at stars. Bukowski was in close proximity to wealth and glamour but he was not a part of it. East Hollywood was, in fact, a seedy district of cheap apartment buildings, sleazy bars and liquor stores with grills over the windows. In the summer it was hot, dusty and dirty, suffocating under smog that settled in this part of this city. There were no movie stars on North Mariposa, just working people and those who had lost their way in society.

At night there would be loud fights, the screeching of car tires, screaming, wild gun shots. Bukowski conjured up the atmosphere of East Hollywood in many poems including 'The Night They Took Whitey' which describes the death of an old man who lived in the same apartment building.

At 4 a.m., Whitey begins haemorrhaging blood and screams for help. Bukowski tries to make the old man comfortable, and then attempts to raise the landlady …

… I beat on the landlady's door
(she is as French as the best wine but tough as
an American steak) and
I hollered her name, *Marcella! Marcella!*
(the milkman would soon be coming with his
pure white milk bottles like chilled lilies)
Marcella! Marcella! help me help me help me,
and she screamed back through the door:
you polack bastard, are you drunk again?

EAST HOLLYWOOD

Bukowski sits down at his 'typer' in his little rented room in East Hollywood. Beside him on his typing table are copies of The Outsider, *the small literary magazine that started publishing his work in 1961.*
(COURTESY OF LOUISE 'GYPSY LOU' WEBB)

FACING PAGE

This is the rooming house at 1623 North Mariposa Avenue, Hollywood, where Bukowski lived between 1958 and 1964. He wrote his grief poems about Jane Cooney Baker when he was here, and many of the letters later collected in Screams from the Balcony. The windows of the apartment Bukowski lived in are circled.

(PHOTOGRAPH BY HOWARD SOUNES)

LEFT

The corridor outside the door to Room 303 at the N. Mariposa rooming house.

(PHOTOGRAPH BY HOWARD SOUNES)

ABOVE

The entrance to the N. Mariposa building. Bukowski met FrancEyE – the mother of his only child – here one night when she arrived by taxi from the bus station downtown. 'Bukowski seemed like this giant, this gorgeous giant,' she says. 'His hair was all slicked back … His gaze was very direct. He had a very symmetrical face. His nose was kind of smashed, but I just thought he was gorgeous.'

(PHOTOGRAPH BY HOWARD SOUNES)

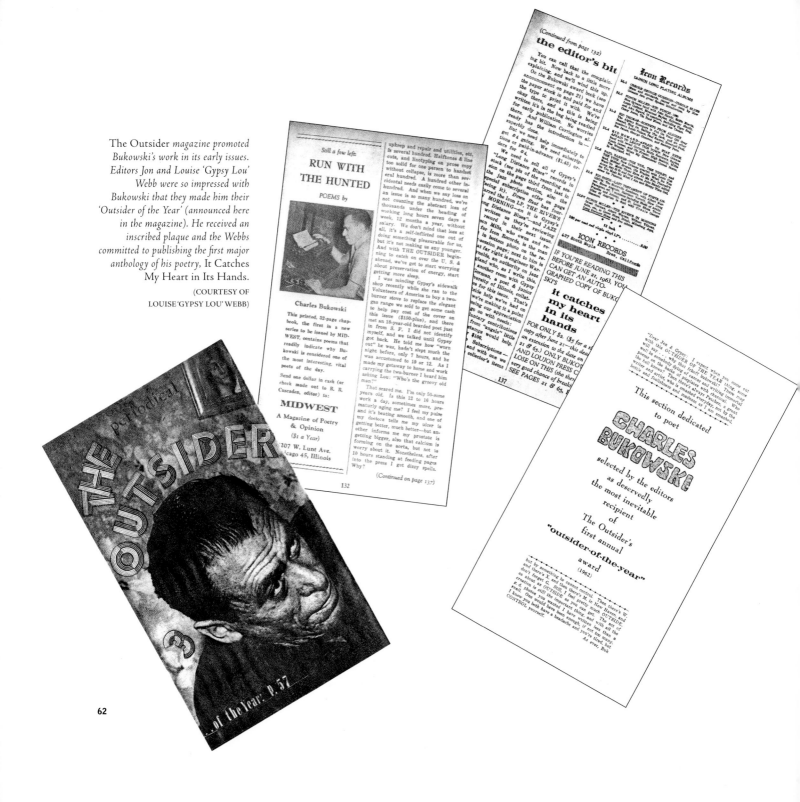

The Outsider *magazine promoted Bukowski's work in its early issues. Editors Jon and Louise 'Gypsy Lou' Webb were so impressed with Bukowski that they made him their 'Outsider of the Year' (announced here in the magazine). He received an inscribed plaque and the Webbs committed to publishing the first major anthology of his poetry, It Catches My Heart in Its Hands.*

(COURTESY OF
LOUISE 'GYPSY LOU' WEBB)

Still a few left:

RUN WITH THE HUNTED

POEMS by

Charles Bukowski

This printed, 32-page chapbook, the first in a new series to be issued by MIDWEST, contains poems that readily indicate why Bukowski is considered one of the most interesting, vital poets of the day.

Send one dollar in cash (or check made out to R. R. Cuscaden, editor) to:

MIDWEST
A Magazine of Poetry & Opinion
($1 a Year)

207 W. Lunt Ave.
Chicago 45, Illinois

upkeep and repair and utilities, etc, is several hundred. Halftones & line cuts, and linotyping on prose copy too solid for one person to handset without collapse, is more than several hundred. A hundred other incidental needs easily come to several hundred. And when we say loss on an issue is so many hundred, we're not counting the abstract loss of thousands under the heading of working long hours seven days a week, 12 months a year, without salary. We don't mind that loss at all, it's a self-inflicted one for us, doing something pleasurable for us, but it's not making us any younger. And with THE OUTSIDER beginning to catch on over the U. S. & abroad, we've got to start worrying about preservation of energy, start getting more sleep.

I was minding Gypsy's sidewalk shop recently while she ran to the Volunteers of America to buy a two-burner stove to replace the elegant gas range we sold to get some cash to help pay cost of the cover on this issue ($150-plus), and there met an 18-year-old bearded poet just in from S. F. I did not identify myself, and we talked until Gypsy got back. He told me how "worn out" he was, hadn't slept much the night before, only 7 hours, and he was accustomed to 10 or 12. As I made my getaway to home and work carrying the two-burner I heard him asking Lou: "Who's the groovy old man?"

That scared me. I'm only 50-some years old. Is this 12 to 16 hours work a day, sometimes more, prematurely aging me? I feel my pulse and it's beating smooth, and one of my doctors tells me my ulcer is getting better, much better—but another informs me my prostate is getting bigger, also that calcium is forming on the aorta, but not to worry about it. Nonetheless, after 10 hours standing at feeding press into the press I get dizzy spells. Why?

132

(Continued on page 137)

(Continued from page 132)

the editor's bit

You can call that the complaining bit. Now back to a little more explaining. and we'll wind this up.

On the Bukowski award book (see announcement on page 21) we have the paper stock in and paid for and the type to print it with. We're okay there, and as this is being written it's in the bag being readied for early publication. No worries there. And William Corrington already has the introduction all superbly done.

But we need help immediately to get #4 going. We need subscriptions or paid-in-advance orders for #4, and to sell all of Gypsy's stock (see pix of the recording session on the page third from last in the jazz photo section also facing it). Down Beat has four-starred the Icon LP. THE RIVER'S MY MORNING, it is Gypsy's "Long Distance Blues" and JAZZ written us they're reviewing record in their next issue.

Jon Mills, who owns and runs for Icon Records, is the man in bottom photo on the session page; next to him is far right to engineer War-arnold, an authority on jazz England who, as I write this, Norman, a poet with Gypsy versity of Illinois, collaborated for this issue. That's we're making it a point beside help we've had on go on with needs: luntary contributions from "angels" would help. $100. Subscriptions and with one we collector's items

Icon Records

12-INCH LONG PLAYING ALBUMS

[list of records]

100 per cent red virgin vinyl LP's ...... 12 each

ICON RECORDS 5.00
427 South Maple
Ross, California

IF YOU'RE READING THIS BEFORE JUNE 21, 1963, YOU CAN GET AN AUTO-GRAPHED COPY OF BUKOW-SKI'S

it catches my heart in its hands

FOR ONLY $2. ($5 for a copy after June 21—this deal an extension to the date on 21 & 65.) ONLY BUKOW AND LOUJON PRESS C LOSE ON THIS (the ther very good chance of breaking SEE PAGES 21 & 65,

137

This section dedicated
to poet

CHARLES BUKOWSKI

selected by the editors
as deservedly
the most inevitable
recipient
of
The Outsider's
first annual
"outsider-of-the-year"
award
(1962)

"Dear Jon & Gypsy, I expect when you come out with this OUTSIDER OF THE YEAR thing how you will say — why that joker, Bukowski? There may well be somebody dying of cancer, some immortal poems on the backs of playing cards, a great writer and artist who is smashed everyday, by the hell of it. Then there's always Patchen, a writer and artist who is smashed and madness as I am, a little and foolishness and

but by something he cannot control. Then there's W. and there's G. and then they're in New Haven, and don't forget C. Still I feel I'm pretty much OUTSIDE as about as OUTSIDE as you can get OUTSIDE. creation is still the important thing, and with all of it all, photos you have I have written less and with of it all. One would have been enough, if not too many. I know you both have a headache and you're tired, but CONTROL yourself.
As ever, Buk"

62

Jon and 'Gypsy Lou' Webb were an eccentric couple from New Orleans who decided Bukowski was a major talent. They featured his work in their small literary magazine, The Outsider, and then published two major anthologies of his poetry – It Catches My Heart in Its Hands and Crucifix in a Deathhand. Although these were only produced in limited editions, they were beautifully printed and helped establish Bukowski's career. Here Bukowski is seen meeting Jon and Gypsy Lou on a trip they made to Los Angeles in August, 1964.

(PHOTOGRAPHS COURTESY OF LOUISE 'GYPSY LOU' WEBB)

One of Bukowski's main correspondents while he was living at N. Mariposa Avenue was writer and academic John William Corrington. He taught literature in Louisiana and wrote a glowing preface for Bukowski's book, It Catches My Heart in Its Hands. They corresponded for several years in the warmest terms before actually meeting, at the home of Jon and Louise Webb, in March 1965. At this meeting Bukowski picked a belligerent argument which ended the friendship.

(PHOTOGRAPH COURTESY OF JOYCE CORRINGTON)

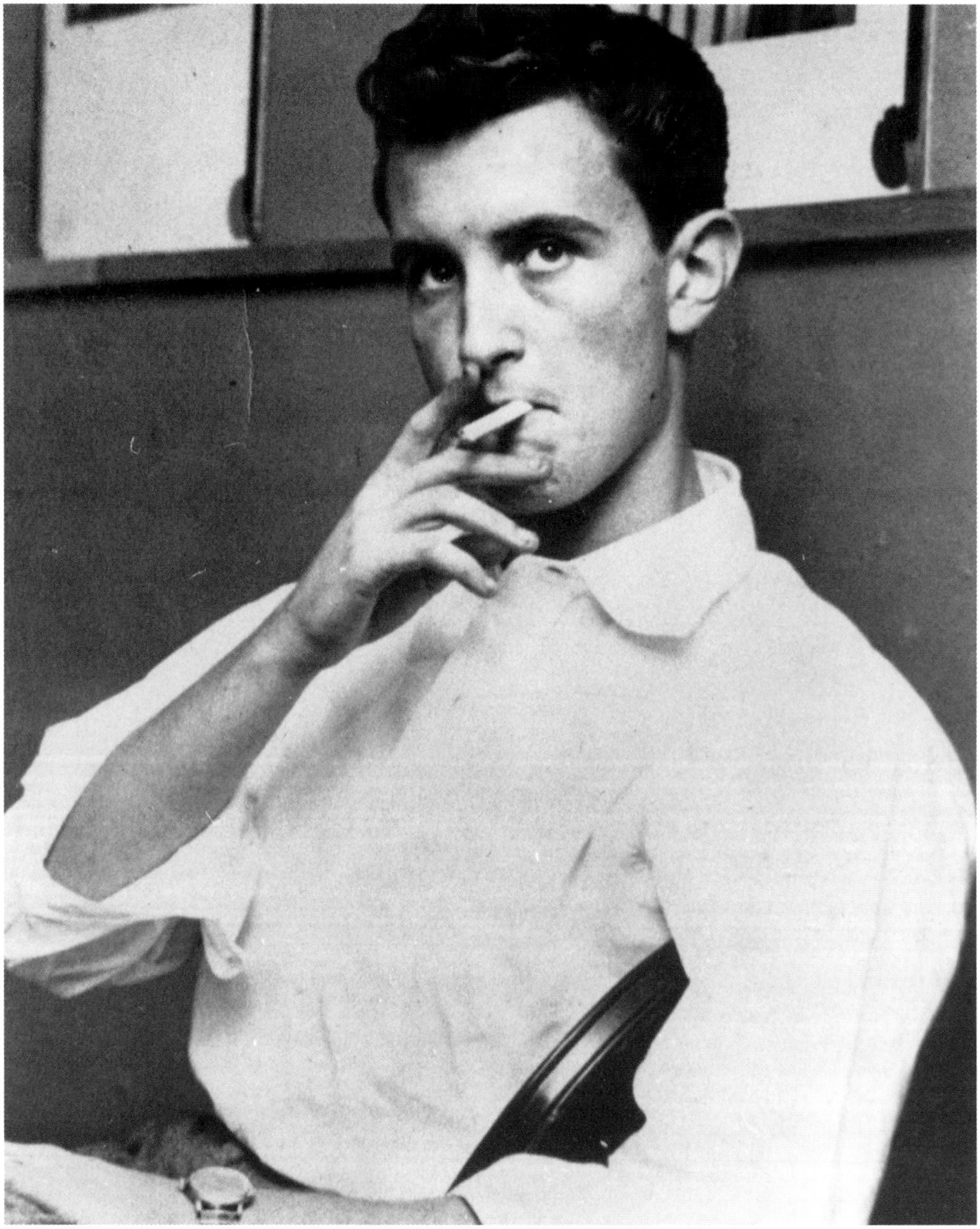

64

Here is a selection of some of the very early chapbooks in which Bukowski's work was published. The poor quality of the printing reflects the amateurish nature of these mimeographed publications. The rarest chapbook here is Flower, Fist and Bestial Wail, published in 1960 by Hearse Press. Only two hundred were printed. The cover for Longshot Pomes for Broke Players (7 Poets Press, 1962) features a drawing by Bukowski. Cold Dogs in the Courtyard (Literary Times-Cyfoeth Press, 1965) was a collection of oddments rejected by other publishers.

The flyer shows that Run with the Hunted cost one dollar, including postage, when it was published in 1962. A copy in good condition would now be worth many hundreds of dollars.

Bukowski was not paid for most of these books. The most he could expect was free copies to give away to friends.

(PHOTOGRAPHS BY DON KLEIN)

The junction of Hollywood Boulevard and Western Avenue (see here in the main picture) is the nucleus of East Hollywood. Bukowski drank in bars in this area, including The Frolic Room (photo inset). Prostitutes walked the streets, and police sirens would wail night and day. In the distance one can see the Hollywood Hills.

(PHOTOGRAPHS BY HOWARD SOUNES)

PREVIOUS PAGES
East Hollywood by night.

(PHOTOGRAPHS BY HOWARD SOUNES)

69

Work is one of the most important themes of Bukowski's writing. He worked various manual jobs until the age of forty-nine, and resented virtually every minute of it. He considered that his real life was in bars, at the race track and at home. With beer in the refrigerator and a symphony on the radio, his spirit would fly he pecked away at the typewriter. Leaving all this to go to his job made him profoundly miserable, as he wrote in 'nature poem':

I could not go to work
tonight because I could not
stop living

Although he worked at his poems constantly Bukowski made no money from his writing until the mid-1960s. He had to have a regular job to survive.

In the early part of his life he worked mostly as a shipping clerk or stock room boy in small factories and stores. The jobs ended when he was fired for absenteeism or when he could not be bothered to come in.

He first worked for the United States Postal Service as a temporary mail carrier in December 1950. As he wrote in his seminal novel *Post Office*, it began as a mistake ...

It was Christmas season and I learned from the drunk up the hill, who did the trick every Christmas, that they would hire damned near anybody, and so I went and the next thing I knew I had this leather sack on my back ...

There was a gap between this Christmas job and March 1952 when Bukowski became a regular carrier with the postal service for $1.61 an hour. He held the job until 1955 when he was forced to leave due to ill health. He later re-applied and became a full-time sorting clerk in January 1958. Although he hated the work, the postal service provided regular employment and a pension. Bukowski would soon be forty and he was frightened of ending his days in poverty.

He worked as postal clerk for the next twelve years, mostly on night shifts so he had time in the day to go to the horse-races at Hollywood Park. It was hard work, sorting a never-ending stream of mail against the clock, with supervisors urging him to work faster. Over the years Bukowski developed chronic back and shoulder pains, and the job severely depressed him. He rarely spoke during his shift, just doggedly doing his work, and leaving as soon as possible.

He would work two weeks straight at the job so he could have long four-day weekends to drink, gamble and write.

As the years went by Bukowski was published in an increasing number of literary magazines and in many privately printed chapbooks. Eventually he was discovered by a young businessman, John Martin, who decided to launch a publishing company, Black Sparrow Press, just to publish Bukowski.

As part of his now burgeoning writing career, Bukowski contributed an outrageous weekly column, 'Notes of a Dirty Old Man', to underground newspapers in Los Angeles. This column came to the attention of the postal service and his supervisors called in the FBI to investigate whether Bukowski – as an employee of a government department – was a dangerous subversive. His supervisors wanted to force him out of his job, anyway, because of his surly attitude and his absenteeism. Finally he was informed he was about to be fired. At this point John Martin stepped in and offered Bukowski $100 a month for life if he would write full-time for Black Sparrow Press. Bukowski took the deal and wrote his great first novel, *Post Office*.

SHIT JOBS

Bukowski worked for the United States Postal Service first as a temporary mail carrier and then as a sorting clerk. As a clerk, he worked here at the gigantic Terminal Annex building in downtown Los Angeles between 1958 and 1970.
(PHOTOGRAPH BY HOWARD SOUNES)

While he was at N. Mariposa Avenue Bukowski met Frances Dean, a divorcee who later changed her name to FrancEyE. Together they had one child, Marina Louise, born 7 September 1964.
(COURTESY OF FRANCEYE)

72

FOR YOUR SAFETY'S SAKE
NEVER ATTEMPT TO DISLODGE
A JAM IN A CONVEYOR BELT
WHILE IT IS RUNNING

FOR YOUR SAFETY'S SAKE
WATCH THE OVERHEAD

LEFT

*Although Bukowski did not marry
FrancEyE they decided to live
together with their daughter and
moved here to 5126 De Longpre
Avenue, Hollywood, in 1964.*

(PHOTOGRAPH BY JOE WOLBERG)

BELOW LEFT

*This is the sorting office in
downtown LA that Bukowski
wrote about in* Post Office.

(PHOTOGRAPH BY HOWARD
SOUNES)

INSETS, ABOVE

*These signs were given to
employees at the Terminal Annex
building, the post office where
Bukowski worked as a mail clerk.*

(FROM THE COLLECTION OF
HOWARD SOUNES)

RIGHT

*Bukowski's landlord at De Longpre
Avenue was Francis Crotty (man with
hat). His wife Grace (middle figure)
became very fond of Bukowski. The
young woman on the right is neighbour
and friend Sina Taylor.*

(FROM THE COLLECTION OF HOWARD
SOUNES)

INSET RIGHT

*Bukowski's outrageous 'Notes of a
Dirty Old Man' column, first
published by the LA underground
magazine* Open City *(see left),
became so popular that it was collected
in book form. This City Lights edition
was published in 1973.*

(PHOTOGRAPH BY DON KLEIN/
COURTESY OF CITY LIGHTS)

BUKOWSKI

NOTES of a DIRTY OLD MAN

One of Bukowski's great passions in life was gambling on horse racing. When he was working at the post office he believed he might be able to become so good at laying bets that he could give up his job and become a professional gambler.
(PHOTOGRAPH BY JOE WOLBERG)

Before each race Bukowski would carefully study the daily Racing Form, handicapping horses. He liked to sit away from the crowds in a quiet part of the stand.

(PHOTOGRAPH BY JOE WOLBERG)

75

Hollywood Park, near Los Angeles International Airport, was the race track Bukowski visited most often. But he would also drive to tracks outside the city.

(PHOTOGRAPH BY JOE WOLBERG)

Studying the form ...
(PHOTOGRAPH BY JOE WOLBERG)

78

... and laying his money down.
(PHOTOGRAPH BY JOE WOLBERG)

MAIN PICTURE

Bukowski's refrigerator.

(PHOTOGRAPH BY JOE WOLBERG)

INSETS

While Bukowski was working for the United States Postal Service he was under investigation by the FBI as a possible subversive within a government organization. These are some of the pages from his recently declassified FBI file.

(FROM THE COLLECTION OF HOWARD SOUNES)

FACING PAGE

In 1970 Bukowski met a feisty young sculptress from Utah named Linda King and began a tempestuous relationship.

(PHOTOGRAPH BY TONY LANE)

OVERLEAF

This photograph was taken at De Longpre Avenue in October 1972, outside the entrance to Bukowski's bungalow. On the left is Bukowski's girlfriend Linda King, with her daughter Clarrissa. On the right is John Martin, the Christian Scientist businessman who fell in love with Bukowski's work and founded the remarkable Black Sparrow Press. Their relationship changed Bukowski's life.

(PHOTOGRAPH BY GERARD MALANGA)

80

When Bukowski finally left the post office, in January 1970, he sat down at his desk at De Longpre Avenue and wrote Post Office – his first and maybe his greatest novel.
This is page one of the manuscript. Notice how Bukowski went through the typescript with pen, deleting words, tightening his sentences. He was originally going to begin the novel, 'It all began as a mistake.'
Behind the type-written page is a piece of paper on which Bukowski jotted ideas for the title of the novel. As you can see he considered Death of Betty, 12 Years Gone and Postal News before settling on Post Office.

1.

It began as a mistake.

It was Christmas season and I learned from the drunk up the hill, who did the trick every Christmas, that they would hire damned near anybody, and so I went and the next thing I knew I had this leather sack on my back and was hiking around at my leisure. What a job, I thought. Soft! They only gave you a block or 2 and if you managed to finish, the regular carrier would give you another block to carry, or maybe you'd go back in and the soup would gave you another, but you just took your time and shoved those Xmas cards in the slots.

I think it was my second day as a Christmas temp that this big woman came out and walked around with me as I delivered my letters. What I meant by big was that her ass was big and her tits were big and that she was big in all the right places. She seemed a bit crazy but I kept looking at her body and I didn't care.

She just talked and talked and talked. Then it came out. Her husband was an officer on an island far away and she got lonely, you know, and lived in this little house in back all by herself.

"What little house?" I asked.

She wrote the address on a piece of paper.

"I'm lonely too," I said, "I'll come by and we'll talk tonight."

I was shacked but the shackjob was gone half the time, off somewhere, and I was lonely all right. I was lonely for that big ass standing beside me.

"All right," she said, "see you tonight."

She was a good one all right, she was a good lay but like all lays after the 3rd. or 4th. night I began to lose interest and didn't go back.

But I couldn't help thinking, god, all these mailmen do is drop in their letters and get laid. This is the job for me, oh yes yes yes.

LEFT
The first edition of Post Office.
(PHOTOGRAPH BY DON KLEIN)

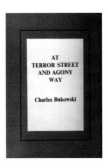

ON GOING OUT TO GET THE MAIL

the droll noon
where squadrons of worms creep up like
stripteasers
to be raped by blackbirds

I go outside
and all up and down the street
the green armies shoot color
like an everlasting 4th. of July,
and I too seem to swell inside,
a kind of unknown bursting, a
feeling, perhaps, that there isn't any
enemy
anywhere

and I reach down into the box
and there is
nothing — not even a
letter from the gas co. saying they will
shut it off
again.

not even a short note from my x-wife
bragging upon her present
happiness.

my hand searches the mailbox in a kind of
disbelief long after the mind has
given up.

there's not even a dead fly
down in there.

I am a fool, I think, I should have known it
works like this.

I go inside as all the flowers leap to
please me.

anything? the woman
asks.

nothing, I answer, what's for
breakfast?

Charles Bukowski
--Charles Bukowski

Printed May, 1966 in Los Angeles by Philip Klein for The Black Sparrow Press.
This edition is limited to thirty copies; three copies lettered a, b and c, which
are not for sale, and twenty seven numbered copies, for sale, all signed by the
poet. This is copy No. 19

*Black Sparrow Press was launched
with a series of simple broadsides
of Bukowski's poetry. Bukowski
was surprised and impressed when
John Martin paid him money in
advance for the right to publish his
work. It was the start of a long
and important relationship. Early
books published included At
Terror Street and Agony Way
and The Days Run Away Like
Wild Horses Over the Hills.
John's wife, Barbara Martin,
designed the covers of the books,
using simple lines and clear
typography.*

(PHOTOGRAPHS BY DON KLEIN)

ABOVE

Bukowski poses with Joe Wolberg and Linda King before the 1972 City Lights reading. He was drinking hard to get his courage up and was physically sick in the street just after this picture was taken. Joe Wolberg worked for City lights and became a friend of Bukowski's.

(COURTESY OF JOE WOLBERG)

RIGHT

After he stopped working as a mail clerk Bukowski became very frightened that he would not be able to make a living as a writer. It was this fear that drove him to give public readings. He would be sick with nerves before hand, but was a natural performer, delighting his audiences with jokes and a curmudgeonly drunk act that was reminiscent of WC Fields. This photograph was taken at one of his most famous readings - an event organized by City Lights in San Francisco in September 1972.

(PHOTOGRAPH BY JOE WOLBERG)

Women had shown little or no interest in Charles Bukowski throughout most of his adult life. He was not a very attractive proposition – strange-looking, often drunk, frequently unemployed and lacking any ambition to have a regular career, to buy a home and start a family. In fact, he ridiculed these ambitions, saying it would make him puke to live such a life. Women left him alone, and there were many years when he had no sex life at all.

But as Bukowski started to become successful as a writer, after he left the post office, women flocked around him. These women were charmed by his honest writing and excited by his burgeoning celebrity. When they got to know him, they were also captivated by his singular personality. Although he could be boorish and aggressive when drunk, Bukowski was for the most part a quiet and sensitive man who, as Linda King says, was unusually open to love. He would plunge into relationships with the enthusiasm of an adolescent. He composed wonderful long love letters, often writing to the same woman several times in one day, and would burst into tears when he was rejected.

Linda King was the first and most important girlfriend of Bukowski's middle age. A sculptress from Utah, she fell in love with Bukowski while making a sculpture of his head. Bukowski loved Linda dearly, but he could not resist the temptation of other women.

Liza Williams was a record company executive Bukowski met through the underground magazines. They went away on holiday together to the island of Catalina during Linda King's annual summer vacation to Utah.

Pamela Miller was a red-headed bar maid who drove Bukowski wild with desire. He wrote lusty poems about her and was crazed with jealousy when he thought she was seeing other men.

There were many other girlfriends, women who read his *Notes of a Dirty Old Man* column and wrote to him asking if they could meet. He would reply by asking them to send a photograph of themselves. Bukowski kept a listed number in the Hollywood telephone directory into the late 1970s. It was another good way of meeting women. As he wrote in his poem, 'how come you're not unlisted?'...

for a man of 55 who didn't get laid
until he was 23
and not very often until he was 50
I think I should stay listed
via Pacific Telephone
until I get as much as
the average man has had.

When Linda King found out about Bukowski's infidelities she became enraged and they had spectacular fights. During one of these fights, Bukowski punched Linda so hard he broke her nose. Another time she drove her car at him. These and other incidents from his love life were recorded in Bukowski's novel, *Women*, and his poetry anthology, *Love Is a Dog from Hell*.

LOVE IS A DOG FROM HELL

Bukowski and Linda King.
(COURTESY OF LINDA KING)

RIGHT

Linda King was a young sculptress with a passionate nature. She met Bukowski in 1970 when he agreed to let her make a sculpture of his head. They began a tempestuous relationship that lasted into the mid-1970s. The sculpture became symbolic of their relationship. When they were together, Bukowski would proudly display it at his home. When he was fighting with Linda, she would take it back.

(PHOTOGRAPH BY TONY LANE)

BELOW RIGHT

Bukowski poses with his sculpture, shortly after it was completed. He and Linda King fell in love while she was making the head. It was later cast in bronze and bought by Bukowski collectors.

(COURTESY OF LINDA KING)

FAR RIGHT

Linda King with some of her other sculptures.

(COURTESY OF LINDA KING)

92

May 25, 1971

My Darling Insane Lover,

I just had to write and tell you how much I love your crazy ass. You are just beautiful. I've never met a man with so much energy and inventivness. You are something else, Bukowski. Originality in the form of a man. And you wonder why I love your mug, well, it's because you are inside of it. You can't help the face you were born with and besides Tully thinks it's beautiful. What you don't understand about me is that I'm all screwed up and things other people think are beautiful I think are ugly. Like ugly to me. I can't understand why women got to the beauty shop and sit for hours to make themselves look ugly. I like old houses new car, new houses, crisp clothes, just set hair does they are all with the paint chiping and bums and weather beaten anything. Listen, Bukowski, you are starting to look pretty good. You've got your belly off, your black heads are all gone, your muscles are growing. You might be getting too good looking for me. I'll have to pass you along to one of those beautiful creatures who model for playboy magazine. This is bullshitting. How can one bull and look what I'm doing. Listen, Bukowski, forget what I said...I love your crazy ass, even thought it doesn't have much heads anymore. Wait let me start again. At about five two and a half I started missing you. I have been missing you for over It is almost seven so it means I've been missing you over hear so I c an hour. I don't like this. Your kisses are very addictive and I have on you awhile. Your kisses are like some people need an upper. I some every few hours like some people need an upper. I help if I call you up and talk, but it's not as good as I got a little mad at you at that party, but you m so much that I've got to forgive you everything. There better than a man that can make you laugh. Nobody can that your wildness is too much, well, I'm convince tha too drunk, but still I have to love all the original up with. You're great, Bukowski. Just great. You a some waves together. It It's like screwin how I get ahold of things. There is one thing about you get better and better. And sometimes it's hard to get you off pro-Bukowski and sometimes it's hard to get you off when you've been drinking a lot. How can anyone el it. YOUR THE GREATEST BUKOWSKI. Do you think I w to tell you how great you are when you're saying it love of the second greatest? Ofcourse not. Think you.

Look, Bukowski, I have just finished a chap the best most honest account of shock treatment too much, not too little, just telling it like i bubbles and life. I'm full of something that is Don't under-estimate the power of woman, Bukows comes in a smaller package. I keep my eyes op think it's necessary anymore. While you're t registering. I'm registering reactio the current and the undercurrent. Something

just sit back and see. All the snarl and growl is going into something with power. XXXXXXX Something's going to give. Who's going to need Sam and his petty ix three or four thousand. Even if I become a scrub woman on skid row you'll need XX Sam and his money mind. There something else, Bukowski...something else tha you men don't want to hail. You XXXXXXXXXXXXX women to fall on their faces. It's alright to screw ng as they XXXX don't make it. If they make it it's r the ego. God, now look what I'm doing in this love m starting a fight. Look, Bukowski, man, I love your. But, I'm proud XXXXXXXX and XXXXXXX I won't sit itutation just because I'm suppose to be the woman. thing wrong with McKlowski's wife. XXXXXXXXXX She's her own steam and image. I'm a Goddamn good kowski and I'll most likely stick to the things d at. You've got your ways of putting women block. I don't miss it or forget it and it rcle one of these days and you'll get chopped spot you've did chopped before. I'm not ou get away with anything, my insane lover get very convinced about my keeping my place, nning wild yourself. Women are cunning and k and they listen and the watch and then t might take them one XXXXXXX planned chop haphazard XXXXX. And then things even out of a woman who actually work at tit for a They are used to Tit tit tit tat. to be on their toes. But personally ng. The man and woman

ABOVE

A letter from Linda to Bukowski complaining about his friendship with rival girlfriend, Liza Williams.

(COURTESY OF LINDA KING)

LEFT

Bukowski's face was like a living sculpture.

(PHOTOGRAPHY BY TONY LANE)

RIGHT

As he became better known, the beer bottle became a regular prop for photographs.

(PHOTOGRAPH BY BRAD DARBY)

FACING PAGE

This is Linda King's former home on Edgewater Terrace, in the Silver Lake suburb of Los Angeles. Bukowski lived here during part of their relationship. He was dragged away by police one night when, during a drunken fight, he threatened to throw a sofa through the window.

(PHOTOGRAPH BY HOWARD SOUNES)

INSET

In this open letter, dated June 1976, Linda King listed all the times that Bukowski had been violent to her. She wrote it in the style of a prosecution case as if Bukowski was on trial.

(COURTESY OF LINDA KING)

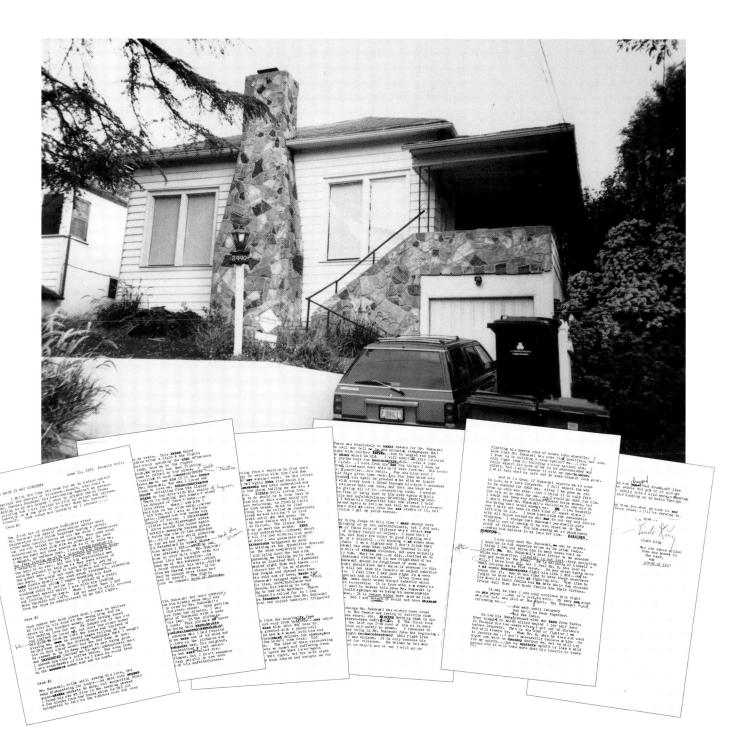

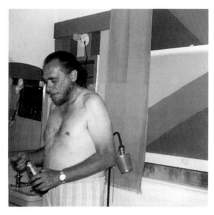

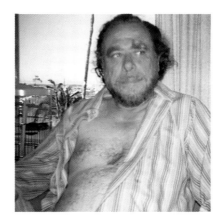

In his entire life, this may have been the only conventional vacation Bukowski ever went on. It took place in July 1972. Linda King was away in Utah for her annual vacation and her rival Liza Williams decided to take Bukowski to the resort island of Catalina, just off the coast of California. They stayed in the Hotel Monterey in the port town of Avalon from 23–30 July. Liza remembers that Bukowski was bemused and confused, not knowing quite how he should behave on vacation. He had no interest in going to the beach, or looking at the sights, and in the end he settled down in the hotel room with some beer and wrote poems. He spent so much time in the room on his own that Liza bought him a caged bird to keep him company. Bukowski and Liza broke up soon after they returned to LA.

(PHOTOGRAPHS COURTESY OF LIZA WILLIAMS)

99

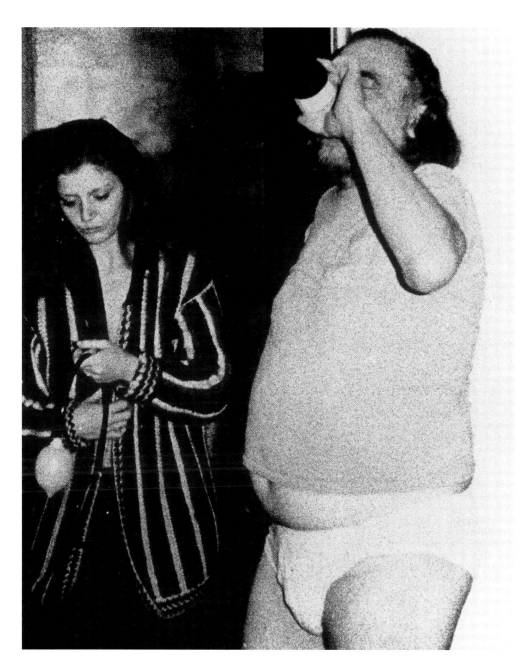

LEFT

As Bukowski became more famous he was invited to give public readings along with other established poets. This 1974 illustration by American artists Dave Geiser shows Bukowski having dinner before a reading in Santa Cruz, California. Around the table one can see writers and poets including Lawrence Ferlinghetti, Allen Ginsberg, Jack Micheline, Shel Silverstein and Gary Snyder. Linda King is depicted because, apart from being a sculptress, she was also a poet of some talent.

(ILLUSTRATION BY DAVE GEISER)

BELOW

Poster for the Santa Cruz reading.

(FROM THE COLLECTION OF HOWARD SOUNES)

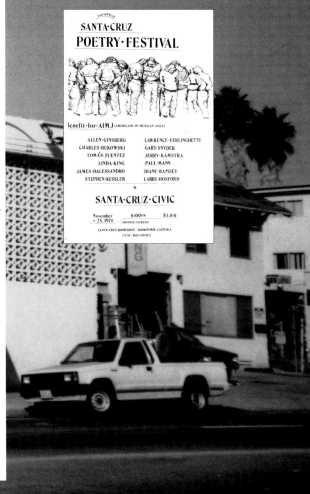

In 1974 Bukowski moved to a new home in a shabby apartment court at 5437 Carlton Way, Hollywood. This was within walking distance of the junction of Hollywood and Western. His neighbours included Brad Darby (left) and Brad's wife Tina (middle). Brad managed a nearby sex shop and Tina worked as a go-go dancer.

(COURTESY OF LINDA KING)

104

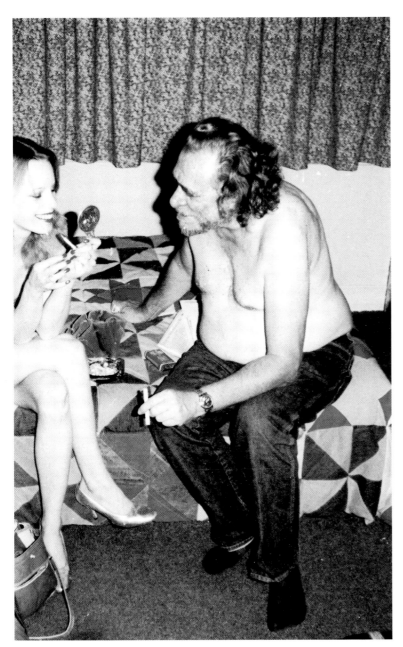

LEFT

Bukowski couldn't help flirting with Tina Darby, much to the disgust of Linda King.

(PHOTOGRAPH BY BRAD DARBY)

ABOVE

This is the sex shop where Brad Darby worked as manager. Bukowski would often visit, sometimes taking magazines home with him. He came to have a nodding acquaintance with the prostitutes who gathered near the store looking for customers.

(PHOTOGRAPH BY HOWARD SOUNES)

CARLOS J. MOORHEAD
20TH DISTRICT, CALIFORNIA

ROOM 1208
LONGWORTH HOUSE OFFICE BUILDING
WASHINGTON, D.C. 20515
(202) 225-4176

COMMITTEE:
JUDICIARY

Congress of the United States
House of Representatives
Washington, D.C. 20515

May 23, 1973

420 N. BRAND BOULEVARD
GLENDALE, CALIFORNIA 91203
(213) 247-8445

125 SOUTH GRAND AVENUE
FEDERAL CENTER
PASADENA, CALIFORNIA 91105

Mr. Charles Bukowski
5124 DeLongpre Avenue
Los Angeles, California 90027

Dear Mr. Bokowski:

I have just had word from the National Endowment
for the Arts that you have obtained a grant in
the amount of $5,000 to assist in furthering your
writing career.

You may have already received notice of this award
but I am pleased to send this information along in
the event you have not heard.

Sincerely yours,

CARLOS J. MOORHEAD
M.C.

CJM:sk

ABOVE
After years of trying, Bukowski
was finally awarded a National
Endowment for the Arts Grant.
(FROM THE COLLECTION OF
HOWARD SOUNES)

RIGHT
Tina Darby, go-go dancer,
neighbour and friend.
(PHOTOGRAPH BY BRAD DARBY)

FAR LEFT
Friend and fellow poet, Ann Menebroker. Bukowski dedicated his book South of No North *to Ann.*
(COURTESY OF ANN MENEBROKER)

LEFT
Friend Joan Smith. Another go-go dancer, she later became a poet and published books about Bukowski including Bukowski Boulevard *(Pearl Editions, 1999).*
(COURTESY OF JOAN SMITH)

BELOW, FAR LEFT
Girlfriend Pamela Miller, immortalised in Women *as the lusty character of Tammie. She was also known to Bukowski as Cupcakes. She is seen here in a 1997 photograph taken by the author.*
(PHOTOGRAPH BY HOWARD SOUNES)

BELOW LEFT
Former girlfriend Amber O'Neil, seen here in a recent photograph. She became the character of Tanya in Women.
(COURTESY OF AMBER O'NEIL)

ABOVE
*The woman on the far left is
Bukowski's girlfriend Joanna Bull.*
(COURTESY OF JOANNA BULL)

RIGHT
*Another female fan and friend, art
student Jo Jo Planteen.*
(COURTESY OF JO JO PLANTEEN)

ABOVE
Bukowski charms an admirer.
(PHOTOGRAPH BY BRAD DARBY)

RIGHT
Bukowski and friend Stella, in Hollywood.
(PHOTOGRAPH BY BRAD DARBY)

Bukowski has a reputation as a misanthrope who shunned company, and it is certainly true that he was contemptuous of mainstream society, but he shared his life with a surprisingly large circle of people.

His family life revolved around his daughter Marina, who was brought up by her mother FrancEyE mostly in Santa Monica, California. Bukowski had little time for FrancEyE, but he doted on Marina.

Bukowski had a lot of girlfriends in his middle years and although he was not someone who ever had a *best* friend, he had many male friends, too, including fellow poets. Bukowski was a prolific correspondent, maintaining long friendships with people, including Canadian poet Al Purdy, whom he had never met. Indeed, he was at his best as a friend when he was able to keep a distance. Poets Douglas Blazek and John William Corrington, both of whom had enjoyed a long and warm correspondence with Bukowski, became disenchanted with him after meeting him in person. He tended to get drunk when he met people for the first time and would test them with sarcastic comments, and bellicose displays of ego. Bukowski also attacked and provoked his friends in writing, peppering his poems and stories with snide comments about friends.

Steve Richmond, a prolific poet and young disciple of Bukowski, was very hurt indeed when Bukowski mocked him in the poem '300 poems':

look, he said, I've written
300 poems in 2
months,
and he handed me the
stack and I
thought
oo oo.

…

what do you think?
he asked?
and I said,
well, some of
these …
but I didn't
finish.

The longest male friendship of Bukowski's life was with his publisher, the Christian Scientist businessman John Martin. The fact that they rarely met helped preserve the friendship. Martin was not around when Bukowski became drunk and belligerent. It also helped that John Martin did not write himself. He was not competition. Bukowski also had respect for the fact that John Martin sent him a check each month, an amount starting at $100 and rising through $7,000-a-month as they sold more books. John Martin would buy him new typewriters and send him parcels of stationery, art supplies, and extra sums of money when he had an urgent bill. And although they didn't see much of each other in person, they exchanged letters almost daily and talked constantly on the telephone. What started as a business arranged changed over the years into a genuine friendship and a kind of partnership. There wouldn't have been a Black Sparrow Press without Bukowski and Bukowski might never have achieved his eventual success if John Martin hadn't been there to support him. 'He used to kid on the phone, 'Is Mr Rolls there?' And I'd say, 'Yes, is this Mr Royce?' says John Martin. 'Because we felt the coming together created something.' When Bukowski married for the second time, in 1985, he chose John Martin as his best man.

HUMANITY, YOU NEVER HAD IT FROM THE BEGINNING

Bukowski with Tales of Ordinary Madness *actor Ben Gazzara (centre) and director Marco Ferreri (left).*
(PHOTOGRAPH BY JOE WOLBERG)

Bukowski with his publisher John Martin, founder of Black Sparrow Press, and Barbara Martin who designs the covers of the books. The relationship between Bukowski and his publisher started as business arrangement and developed into the longest friendship of Bukowski's life, extending over twenty-eight years. During that time Martin developed a profound respect for Bukowski both as a man and a writer. 'One thing about Bukowski: extraordinarily honest man,' says John Martin. 'He hated any kind of dishonesty. He hated deceit. I always said that if I ever wanted to get a perfectly straight answer without any of the person's ego in it, or their prejudices, I would go to Bukowski. He was the only person I have ever known who would tell you honestly, exactly what you asked him.'

(FROM THE COLLECTION OF HOWARD SOUNES)

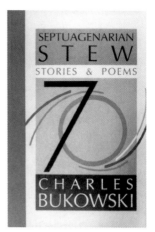

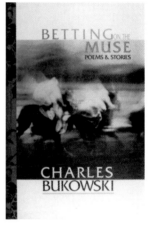

John and Barbara Martin in Barbara's home studio near Santa Rosa, California, in 1997. This is where Barbara designs the Black Sparrow Press covers.

(MAIN PHOTOGRAPH BY HOWARD SOUNES/ OTHER PHOTOGRAPHY BY DON KLEIN)

BLACK SPARROW PRESS

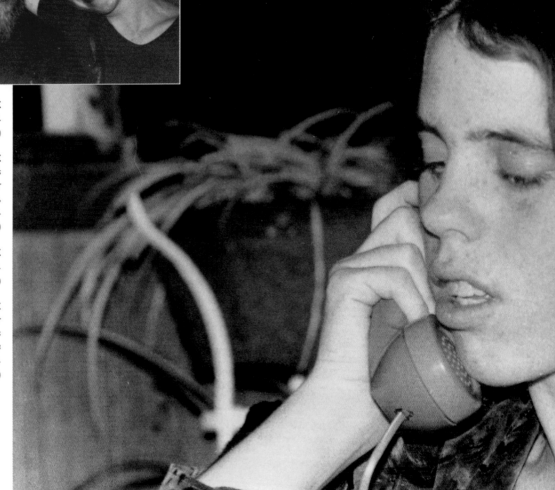

ABOVE
Bukowski with his daughter.
(PHOTOGRAPH BY LINDA KING)

MAIN PICTURE
Marina Louise was Bukowski's only child. She grew up with her mother mostly in Santa Monica, California.
(COURTESY OF FRANCEYE)

INSET, FACING PAGE
Marina as a young woman.
(COURTESY OF FRANCEYE)

FACING PAGE
Bukowski's feelings for his daughter were eloquently expressed in this 1973 poem, published as a broadside by Black Sparrow Press.
(PHOTOGRAPHY BY DON KLEIN)

LOVE POEM
TO MARINA

my girl is 8
and that's old enough to know
better or worse or
anything
so I relax around her and
hear various astounding things
about sex
life in general and life in particular;
mostly it's very
easy
except I became a father when most men
become grandfathers, I am a very late starter
in everything,
and I stretch on the grass and sand
and she rips dandelions up
and places them in my
hair
while I doze in the sea breeze.
I awaken
shake
say, "what the hell?"
and flowers fall over my eyes and over my nose
and over my
lips.
I brush them away
and she sits above me
giggling.

daughter,
right or wrong,
I do love you,
it's only that sometimes I act as if
you weren't there,
but there have been fights with women
notes left on dressers
factory jobs
flat tires in Compton at 3 a.m.,
all those things that keep people from
knowing each other and
worse than
that.

thanks for the
flowers.

CHARLES BUKOWSKI

Charles Bukowski 79/100

Bukowski and his poet friend John Thomas share a beer. When Bukowski was working for the United States Postal Service he would come over to John Thomas' house late at night to talk how unhappy he was at work. The two men remained friends after Bukowski left the post office and Thomas was one of the few old friends who was invited to attend Bukowski's funeral in 1994. On the right is Philomene Long, poet and partner of John Thomas.
(COURTESY OF JOHN THOMAS)

FAR LEFT, TOP

Writer Jory Sherman was an old drinking buddy of Bukowski's from when he lived on North Mariposa Avenue. It was to Sherman that Bukowski went for consolation after Jane Cooney Baker died. The friendship soured when Bukowski became well-known. He responded to Jory Sherman's letters with frosty replies, saying he did not want visitors and implying that they had never been real friends. In 1981 Sherman retaliated by published a scathing pamphlet about Bukowski which he called Bukowski: Friendship, Fame & Bestial Myth *– a play on the title of Bukowski's book,* Flower, Fist and Bestial Wail.

(COURTESY OF JORY SHERMAN)

LEFT

Bob Lind had a pop hit in 1966 with the song 'Elusive Butterfly'. A fan of Bukowski's work, the singer visited the poet at home for a drinking session and was disappointed when Bukowski portrayed him in his novel Women *as the irritating character Dinky Summers.*

(COURTESY OF BOB LIND)

FAR LEFT, MIDDLE

German-born photographer Michael Montfort became a close friend after being sent to photograph Bukowski for a magazine feature.

(PHOTOGRAPH BY HOWARD SOUNES)

FAR LEFT, BOTTOM

Poet Harold Norse was another friend who fell out with Bukowski when he became famous.

(PHOTOGRAPH BY JOE WOLBERG)

RIGHT

Poet Steve Richmond published work by Bukowski in a radical magazine he launched in 1966, called The Earth Rose. *The debut issue had a huge front page headline which read FUCK HATE (below). Richmond was arrested for obscenity.*

(PHOTOGRAPH BY JOE WOLBERG/ THE EARTH ROSE COURTESY OF STEVE RICHMOND)

MAIN PICTURE

Bukowski poses with his Comet car outside the apartment court on Carlton Way, Hollywood. This is where he lived from 1974 to 1978.

(PHOTOGRAPH BY TINA EWING)

the *EARTH ROSE*

FUCK HATE

Whereby, on this day we able minded creators do hereby tell you, the Establishment: FUCK YOU IN THE MOUTH. WE'VE HEARD ENOUGH OF YOUR BULLSHIT.

beings of beauty

118

RIGHT

Poet Neeli Cherkovski was a close friend of Bukowski's for many years. In 1969 they launched a small literary magazine together, Laugh Literary and Man the Humping Guns, *the debut issue of which carried a handwritten manifesto by Bukowski, ' In Disgust with Poetry Chicago ...' The two men drifted apart when Bukowski became famous.*

(PHOTOGRAPH BY HOWARD SOUNES)

BOTTOM

Neeli Cherkovski's father, Sam Cherry, was also friendly with Bukowski. A former hobo, Sam Cherry took the boxcar photograph of Bukowski which was used in the 1969 poetry anthology, The Days Run Away Like Wild Horses Over the Hills.

(PHOTOGRAPH BY HOWARD SOUNES)

FACING PAGE

Poster advertising a Bukowski poetry reading in San Francisco on 31 May 1975.

(FROM THE COLLECTION OF HOWARD SOUNES)

120

city lights poets theater

Bukowski
READS HIS
poetry

SATURDAY

MAY 31 8 pm

telegraph hill gym
555 chestnut (nr. mason)

362-8193

tickets 2. at CITY LIGHTS BOOKSTORE

& CODY'S (berkeley)

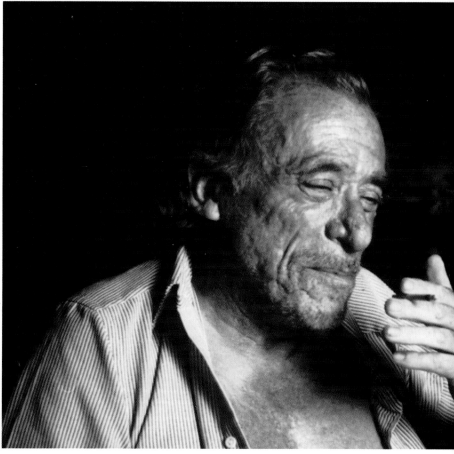

ABOVE LEFT
Canadian poet Al Purdy was much admired by Bukowski.
Their correspondence was published as The Bukowski/
Purdy Letters *in 1983.*
(COURTESY OF AL PURDY)

BELOW LEFT
Small press publisher John Bennett who partied with
Bukowski in San Francisco in the 1970s.
(COURTESY OF JOHN BENNETT)

Bukowski in conversation.
(PHOTOGRAPH BY JOE WOLBERG)

123

After decades of obscurity, and some genuine hardship, Bukowski began to enjoy fame and financial success in the late 1970s.

It was the surprising popularity of his work in Germany that brought in the first substantial royalties. Translations of his work quickly sold more than a hundred thousand copies there, and he was featured in mainstream magazines including the German edition of *Playboy*.

Around the same time Bukowski met a young fan named Linda Lee Beighle. A blonde restaurant owner twenty-three years his junior, she became his constant companion. In 1978 when Bukowski flew to Germany to give a poetry reading, Linda Lee was with him. During the trip they visited Andernach, the Rhineland town of Bukowski's birth, and Bukowski had an emotional reunion with his uncle Heinrich Fett. On his return to the United States, Bukowski moved out of his East Hollywood apartment and raised a mortgage on a comfortable detached home in the port town of San Pedro, south of Los Angeles. Linda Lee began to live there with him. In 1985 she became his second wife.

Money continued to come in from Europe, and from the increasing success of his work in America where his 1978 novel, *Women*, was followed by a very successful novel of childhood, *Ham on Rye*. Black Sparrow Press also published anthologies of poetry and short stories. Bukowski was soon able to pay the mortgage off on his San Pedro home, and later had a swimming pool installed in the garden. When the '67 Volks broke down in 1979, Bukowski bought a new $16,000 BMW. He luxuriated in the car as he drove to the race track, thoroughly enjoying his new found success. He knew that he was a lucky man to have had his work recognised in his life time and he did not feel at all awkward about enjoying success. He expressed these feelings in the poem, 'the luck of the draw':

after decades and decades of poverty
as I now approach the lip of the
grave,
suddenly I have a home, a new car, a
spa, a swimming pool, a computer

will this destroy me?
…

the boys in the jails, the slaughterhouses,
the factories, on the park benches, in the
post offices, the bars
would never believe me
now.

Success attracted the attention of the film industry and two movies were made in the 1980s based on Bukowski's work. Bukowski had no personal involvement in the first film, *Tales of Ordinary Madness*, starring Ben Gazzara. But he wrote the screenplay for the second, *Barfly*, starring Mickey Rourke. The director, Barbet Schroeder, became a close friend. Bukowski also became acquainted with several film actors including Elliott Gould, Sean Penn and Harry Dean Stanton. The boisterous young Penn, then married to Madonna, became a particular friend. 'He liked Sean's brashness, I'm sure,' says Harry Dean Stanton. '[His] talent, and mind.'

The possessions, the films, the celebrity friends all mean little in context. Bukowski's writing remains his great achievement. But the few years of fame and wealth he enjoyed in the latter part of his life were a wonderful and unexpected late reward after decades when hardly anybody knew or cared about his work.

Bukowski's manual typewriter. He wrote with old machines like this for many years, using an electric typewriter and then an Apple Macintosh late in his career.

(PHOTOGRAPH BY JOE WOLBERG)

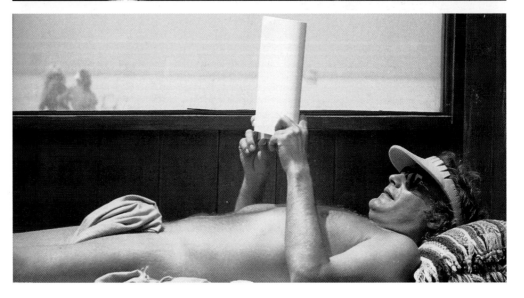

RIGHT
In the movie Barfly *Faye Dunaway played a character based on Jane Cooney Baker and Mickey Rourke played a character based on Bukowski. It is this film that made the general public aware of Bukowski for the first time. He was the bum who had a movie made about his life.*
(PHOTOGRAPH: PEOPLE IN PICTURES)

BELOW
Barfly *director Barbet Schroeder (pictured) also made the remarkable documentary film,* The Charles Bukowski Tapes.
(PHOTOGRAPH BY JOE WOLBERG)

LEFT
Bukowski with the team who made Tales of Ordinary Madness: *actor Ben Gazzara and Italian director Marco Ferreri. The film was released to dismal reviews in 1981.*
(PHOTOGRAPH BY JOE WOLBERG)

BELOW LEFT
Promotional artwork for the film, Tales of Ordinary Madness.
(COURTESY OF ART HOUSE PRODUCTIONS LTD)

BELOW RIGHT
Bukowski at his desk at home in San Pedro in the 1980s.
(COURTESY OF KARL FETT)

FACING PAGE

Bukowski's second wife, Linda Lee Beighle, ran a health food restaurant at Redondo Beach, The Dew Drop Inn. She is seen posing outside the restaurant (left) with Marina Bukowski (right).
(COURTESY OF KARL FETT)

THIS PAGE

When Bukowski made a little money he started eating out at the Musso & Frank Grill on Hollywood Boulevard. This has been a venerable Hollywood institution since 1919, and many great writers dined here over the years including Raymond Chandler and Bukowski's early hero, John Fante. Bukowski liked to eat the lamb special, and drank sweet German white wine. He wrote about the restaurant in two novels, Hollywood *and* Pulp. *The gentleman in the jacket is bar man Ruben Rueda who served Bukowski for many years. When Bukowski died, Mr Rueda cancelled the restaurant's order for sweet German white wine. Bukowski was the only customer who drank it.*
(PHOTOGRAPH BY HOWARD SOUNES)

129

THIS PAGE

As Marina grew up she came to have a strong resemblance to her father.

(PHOTOGRAPHS COURTESY OF KARL FETT)

FACING PAGE

Marina married on 17 October 1989, when she was twenty-four. The groom was a thirty-six-year-old aerospace engineer. Bukowski is seen dancing with his daughter at the reception in Santa Monica, California.

(PHOTOGRAPH BY CONCEPCION TADEO)

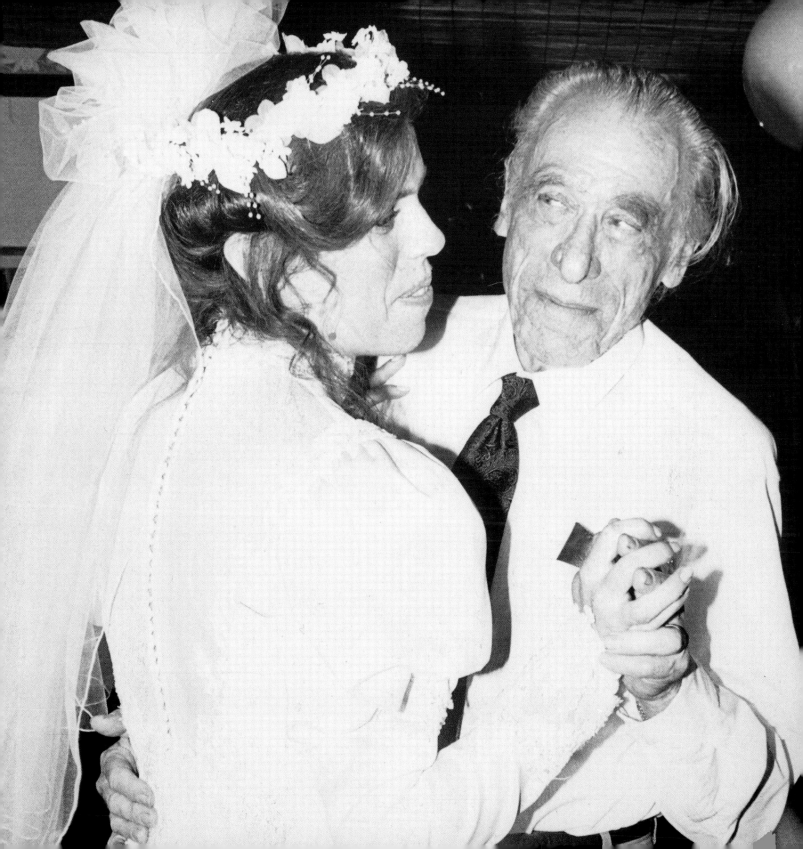

ABOVE
*As he got older, Bukowski became
very fond of stray cats and filled
his house with them. Here is one
of his favourites.*
(PHOTOGRAPH BY JOE WOLBERG)

RIGHT
*Bukowski at home in San Pedro
with one of his cats.*
(PHOTOGRAPH BY JOE WOLBERG)

132

Hello John:

I don't like last title suggested for book of stories, it can
be

READ

WHI

ss.

Not   but
ver   vie
I'm   ed
is
ar

hen
poems

wil
don

y is
t it
rea   , always.
dwe

o.k.,

yr boy,

Film actor Sean Penn became a
close friend of Bukowski, visiting
him at San Pedro. He is seen here
with Linda Lee Bukowski.
(PHOTOGRAPH BY CONCEPCION
TADEO)

CHINASKI,
YOU TURD....

133

As Bukowski became more successful, journalists from across the world came to interview him. Here he talks with Italian critic Fernando Pivano who came to San Pedro in 1980. Watching them is Linda Lee. Note: the mass of empty bottles on the shelf beside the television. Fernando Pivano later published an account of her meeting in Charles Bukowski: Laughing with the Gods (Sun Dog Press, 2000).

(PHOTOGRAPH BY JOE WOLBERG)

Bukowski takes out the trash at San Pedro. Behind him is his '67 Volks, retired by this stage.
(PHOTOGRAPH BY JOE WOLBERG)

136

Bukowski paid $16,000 cash for his new BMW, *astonishing the car salesman.*
(PHOTOGRAPH BY JOE WOLBERG)

COLD DOGS
in the
COURTYARD

by charles bukowski

COLD DOGS
in the
COURTYARD

by charles bukowski

Considering how Bukowski abused his body throughout his life it is remarkable that he lived to the age he did. Heavy smoking, heavier drinking and a lack of any sustained exercise kept him fit and well into his late sixties.

But after the release of *Barfly*, in 1987, Bukowski's health started to decline. He felt ill for much of 1988, assuming for a while that he had the flu. He was eventually diagnosed as having tuberculosis. Much of 1989 was taken up with fighting the illness.

In August 1990 Bukowski began to draw his pension, and Black Sparrow Press published *Septuagenarian Stew* to celebrate his seventieth year. He was feeling better and enjoyed a resurgence in his work in 1991 after he started writing on an Apple Macintosh. The poems flooded out. One of the greatest of his poetry anthologies, *The Last Night of the Earth Poems*, was published in 1992. But his health was beginning to falter again and, after a series of tests, he was informed that he had leukemia.

His habits changed. He lost interest in horse-racing, stopped drinking and spent his days sitting in the garden with his cats. He wrote movingly about death in poems like 'August, 1993':

> musing through those DH Lawrence
> afternoons,
> those horseless days,
> these nights of music trickling from the
> walls,
> this waiting for the fullness and the
> charge.

Shortly before his death Bukowski completed his sixth and last novel. *Pulp* is a pastiche of a hard-boiled detective novel, with characters based on Bukowski and his friends. Bukowski becomes private eye Nicky Belane and John Martin inspired the client, John Barton. Barton hires Belane to find The Red Sparrow. This mysterious creatures appears before Belane at the end of the novel as he lays dying, gunned down in Griffith Park. *Pulp* is not one of Bukowski's better books, being something of a failed experiment, but the fact that Bukowski was contemplating his own death comes through strongly in the closing words of the novel:

> And there I was with that gigantic glowing bird. It stood there.
> This can't be true, I thought. This isn't the way it is supposed to happen. No, this isn't the way it is supposed to happen.
> Then, as I watched, the Sparrow slowly opened its beak. A huge void appeared. And within the beak was a vast yellow vortex, more dynamic than the sun, unbelievable.
> This isn't the way it happens, I thought again.
> The beak opened wide, the Sparrow's head moved closer and the blaze and the blare of yellow swept over and enveloped me.

After undergoing a course of chemotherapy treatment, Charles Bukowski died in San Pedro Peninsula Hospital on 9 March 1994, aged seventy-three.

He was buried not with his parents and grandparents in the family plot at Altadena, but on his own at Green Hills Memorial Park, near San Pedro. The cemetery is laid out with acres of green lawn, with glimpses of the ocean in the distance.

HORSELESS DAYS AND GOODBYE SMILES

FACING PAGE
Charles and Linda Lee Bukowski in Los Angeles in 1991. They were attending a play based on his work, staged to celebrate his seventy-first birthday.
(PHOTOGRAPH BY CONCEPCION TADEO)

FOLLOWING PAGE
Bukowski was a remarkably prolific author. During his lifetime he published more than forty-five books of poetry and prose. If one counts broadsides and other specialist publications, the total of his published works exceeds one hundred and fifty. A selection of his books is arranged here. Note the limited edition book, The Wedding, *published to commemorate Bukowski's wedding to Linda Lee.*
(PHOTOGRAPHY BY DON KLEIN)

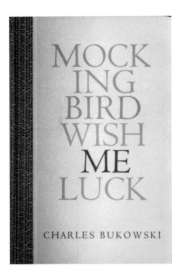

MOCK
ING
BIRD
WISH
ME
LUCK

CHARLES BUKOWSKI

BUKOWSKI

Scarlet

CHARLES
BUKOWSKI

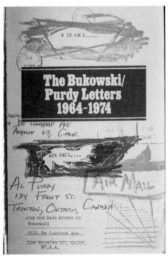

The Bukowski/
Purdy Letters
1964-1974

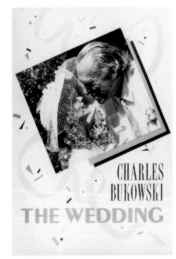

CHARLES
BUKOWSKI

THE WEDDING

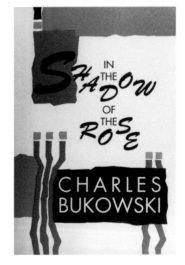

IN
THE
SHADOW
OF
THE
ROSE

CHARLES
BUKOWSKI

CHARLES
BUKOWSKI

TALKING
TO MY
MAILBOX

DANGLING IN THE
TOURNEFORTIA

CHARLES BUKOWSKI

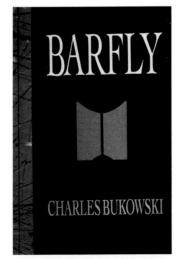

BARFLY

CHARLES BUKOWSKI

There's
No
Business
Charles
Bukowski

ILLUSTRATIONS
BY
R. CRUMB

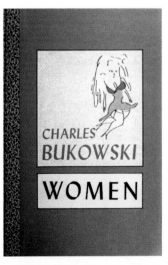

CHARLES
BUKOWSKI

WOMEN

CHARLES
BUKOWSKI

BURNING
IN
WATER
DROWNING
IN
FLAME

SELECTED
POEMS
1955–1973

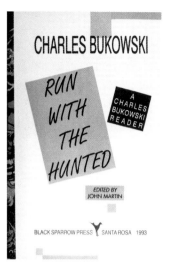

BRING ME YOUR LOVE
CHARLES BUKOWSKI

ILLUSTRATIONS BY R. CRUMB

CHARLES BUKOWSKI

RUN
WITH
THE
HUNTED

A CHARLES BUKOWSKI READER

EDITED BY
JOHN MARTIN

BLACK SPARROW PRESS · SANTA ROSA · 1993

LOVE
IS A
DOG
FROM
HELL

CHARLES
BUKOWSKI

THE DAY IT
SNOWED IN

L.A.

CHARLES BUKOWSKI

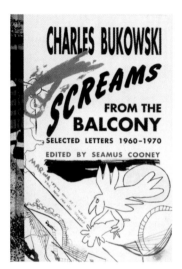

CHARLES BUKOWSKI

SCREAMS
FROM THE
BALCONY
SELECTED LETTERS 1960–1970

EDITED BY SEAMUS COONEY

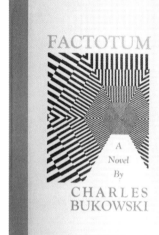

FACTOTUM

A
Novel
By
CHARLES
BUKOWSKI

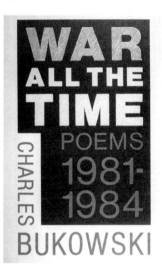

WAR
ALL THE
TIME
POEMS
1981–
1984

CHARLES
BUKOWSKI

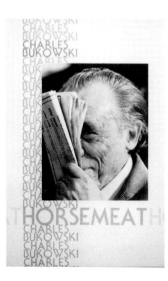

BUKOWSKI
CHARLES
BUKOWSKI
CHARLES
BUKOWSKI
CHARLES
CHARLES
BUKOWSKI
CHARLES
BUKOWSKI
CHARLES
BUKOWSKI
CHARLES
BUKOWSKI

HORSEMEAT

BUKOWSKI

HAM ON RYE

CHARLES BUKOWSKI

Charles
SOUTH
OF NO
NORTH
Bukowski

"**I** WAS SICKENED BY LOOKING AT THOSE FACES, MOST OF THEM SMILING. THE FACES WERE BLAND, EMPTY, VERY HOLLYWOOD, QUITE QUITE HORRIFYING."

In the last years of his life Bukowski kept a daily journal which Black Sparrow Press published in 1997 as The Captain Is Out to Lunch and the Sailors Have Taken Over the Ship. *Artist R. Crumb, who knew Bukowski and illustrated some of his short stories in the 1980s, created these extraordinary illustrations for the book, depicting Bukowski at home in San Pedro in his final years.*

(ILLUSTRATION BY R. CRUMB. THIS AND OTHER R. CRUMB ILLUSTRATIONS CAN BE FOUND IN THE CAPTAIN IS OUT TO LUNCH AND THE SAILORS HAVE TAKEN OVER THE SHIP, BY CHARLES BUKOWSKI, PUBLISHED BY BLACK SPARROW PRESS)

146

R. CRUMB '96

"EASY DAY. GOT IN THE SPA LIKE A BIG TIMER. THE SUN WAS OUT AND THE WATER BUBBLED AND WHIRLED, HOT. I SOOTHED OUT. WHY NOT?"

R. CRUMB '96

147

ABOVE RIGHT
In August 1988 Bukowski was visited by his cousin Katherine Wood (left) and her sister Eleanor. Katherine is the daughter of Bukowski's Uncle John, about whom he wrote the poem 'the bones of my uncle'. They are seen here in the living room of Bukowski's home in San Pedro, California.
(COURTESY OF KATHERINE WOOD)

BELOW RIGHT
Charles and Linda Lee Bukowski at home in San Pedro, during an interview in 1993.
(PHOTOGRAPH BY ROBERT GUMPERT)

148

ABOVE LEFT
Charles and Linda Lee Bukowski.
(PHOTOGRAPH BY
ROBERT GUMPERT)

BELOW LEFT
Bukowski in his work room at San Pedro, the year before his death.
(PHOTOGRAPH BY
ROBERT GUMPERT)

ABOVE
Bukowski's only grandchild, Nikhil
Henry Bukowski Sahoo, who was
born in July 1997.
(COURTESY OF FRANCEYE)

RIGHT
Marina with her son, Nikhil.
(COURTESY OF FRANCEYE)

A bronze cast of Bukowski's head was displayed on a shelf here at the Baroque Book Store in Hollywood. The store was owned by Sholom 'Red' Stodolsky, an irascible old book dealer, very good friend of Bukowski, and the inspiration for the character of Red in the novel Pulp. Red dealt in rare first editions and his store was like a Bukowski museum. In the glass case under the head one can see a first edition of Crucifix in a Deathhand. The poster on the cabinet, Bukowski Lives!, was published by Black Sparrow Press. Red Stodolsky has since died. The store subsequently became a shop selling eye glasses.

MAIN PICTURE

Bukowski was buried here at the
Green Hills Memorial Park,
Rancho Palos Verdes,
on 14 March 1994.

(PHOTOGRAPH BY
HOWARD SOUNES)

INSET, BELOW

The order of service for
Bukowski's funeral.

(FROM THE COLLECTION OF
HOWARD SOUNES)

INSET, FAR RIGHT

Charles Bukowski's grave.

(PHOTOGRAPH BY
CONCEPCION TADEO)

152

Green Hills Mortuary
and
Memorial Chapel
within
Green Hills Memorial Park
27501 South Western Avenue
RANCHO PALOS VERDES, CA. 90732
831-0311

The model for the famous "Praying Hands" by Albrecht Dürer
was a fellow student who gave up his own future as an artist
by working in the fields to support Dürer in his studies.

A legend has grown around this drawing due to it's quiet but
powerful spiritual impact. It is said that the home with a copy
of it will experience peace and tranquility. The inspirational quality
of the art will doubtless help focus the mind on God.

In Memory of

BUT THEY'VE LEFT US A BIT OF MUSIC
AND A SPIKED SHOW IN THE CORNER,
A JIGGER OF SCOTCH, A BLUE NECKTIE,
A SMALL VOLUME OF POEMS BY RIMBAUD,
A HORSE RUNNING AS IF THE DEVIL
WERE TWISTING HIS TAIL
OVER BLUEGRASS AND SCREAMING,
AND THEN,
LOVE AGAIN
LIKE A STREETCAR TURNING THE CORNER
ON TIME,
THE CITY WAITING,
THE WINE AND THE FLOWERS,
THE WATER WALKING ACROSS THE LAKE
AND SUMMER AND WINTER
AND SUMMER AND SUMMER
AND WINTER AGAIN.

CHARLES BUKOWSKI

HANK

BORN

AUGUST 16, 1920

PASSED AWAY

MARCH 9, 1994

SERVICES

3:00 P.M.
MONDAY, MARCH 14, 1994
GREEN HILLS MORTUARY CHAPEL

OFFICIATING

MONK ON

INTERMENT

GREEN HILLS MEMORIAL PARK
SERVICES WILL CONCLUDE AT THE INTERMENT SITE

SOURCE NOTES ON THE TEXT

The text is mostly drawn from the research undertaken for my biography of Bukowski, *Charles Bukowski: Locked in the Arms of a Crazy Life* (Rebel Inc, 1998). Extensive source notes are contained there. Additional sources are listed here:

The Kate Bukowski quotes are from letters in the collection of Karl Fett.

The quote 'making a study on [Linda] … ' is from the second volume of Bukowski's collected letters, *Living on Luck* (Black Sparrow Press, 1995).

The Tina Darby quote 'so he ate … ' is from an interview with the author.

The quote, 'he did not have any intention … ' and other quotes relating to Bukowski's investigation by the FBI are from Bukowski's declassified FBI file (File # 140–35907).

The phrase 'frozen man' is from the thirty-ninth short story in *Notes of a Dirty Old Man* (City Lights, 1969).

The quote 'Most human beings … ' is from *The Charles Bukowski Tapes* (Les Films du Losange, 1987).

The short story 'Confession of a Coward' appears in *Betting on the Muse* (Black Sparrow Press, 1996).

Post Office is published by Black Sparrow Press.

All quotes from John Martin are from interviews with the author, except 'that … coming together … ' which is from the television documentary, *The Ordinary Madness of Charles Bukowski* (BBC, 1995).

The Jon Webb quote 'more than half a hundred … ' is from *The Outsider Vol. 1* (Loujon Press, 1961).

The poem 'marina' appears in *Mockingbird Wish Me Luck* (Black Sparrow Press, 1972).

The poem 'Old man, Dead in a Room' appears in *The Roominghouse Madrigals* (Black Sparrow Press, 1988).

The quote from Linda King 'When I met him … ' is from an interview with the author.

The Taylor Hackford quote 'Carlton Way was sleazy … ' is from an interview with the author.

The poem 'the bluebird' appears in *The Last Night of the Earth Poems* (Black Sparrow Press, 1992).

Hollywood is published by Black Sparrow Press.

The poem 'roll the dice' is from *What Matters Most Is How Well You Walk Through the Fire* (Black Sparrow Press, 1999)

Ham on Rye is published by in the United States by Black Sparrow Press, and in the United Kingdom by Rebel Inc.

The poem 'the bones of my uncle' and 'for Jane' are from *The Days Run Away Like Wild Horses Over the Hills* (Black Sparrow Press, 1969)

The Katherine Wood quotes are from an interview with the author.

'Confessions of a Man Insane Enough to Live With Beasts' appears in *South of No North* (Black Sparrow Press, 1973).

Ask the Dust is published in the United States by Black Sparrow Press and in the United Kingdom by Rebel Inc.

The quote from Francis Billie – 'He was disappointed …' is from an interview with the author.

'The Night They Took Whitey' is from *The Roominghouse Madrigals* (Black Sparrow Press, 1988)

FrancEyE's quote – 'Bukowski seemed like this…' – is from an interview with the author.

'nature poem' and 'the luck of the draw' are published in *Betting on the Muse* (Black Sparrow Press, 1996)

'how come you're not unlisted' is from *Love Is a Dog From Hell* (Black Sparrow Press, 1977)

'300 poems' is from *Mockingbird Wish Me Luck* (Black Sparrow Press, 1972)

The Harry Dean Stanton quote – 'He liked Sean's…' – is from an interview with the author.